PRAYER WORKBOOK
for Hebrew and Heritage 2
Siddur Program

THINK AND THANK

PRISCILLA FISHMAN

BEHRMAN HOUSE

ISBN: 87441-375-3

ILLUSTRATIONS BY ERIKA WEIHS

COVER/BOOK DESIGN BY ROBERT J. O'DELL

MANUFACTURED IN THE UNITED STATES OF AMERICA

INTRODUCTION

The siddur is a collection of prayers to God. This Workbook will help you to understand the words in our prayers. You will learn *why* we pray and *how* we pray as Jews.

Sir Moses Montefiore was a British philanthropist of the nineteenth century. He began his life as a non-practicing Jew, but came to know and love Judaism. He gave practical expression to the mitzvot by extending aid to Jewish communities throughout the world. *Think and Thank* appears on Montefiore's family coat of arms — the same coat of arms that is on the title page of this book.

As you complete the exercises in this Workbook, we hope you will *think* a great deal about God and that you will learn to *thank* God for our wonderful world. That is why we have called it *Think and Thank*.

Let us begin our studies in this new book with a blessing:

בָּרוּךְ אַתָּה ה׳, אֱלֹהֵינוּ מֶלֶךְ הָעוֹלָם,
שֶׁהֶחֱיָנוּ וְקִיְּמָנוּ וְהִגִּיעָנוּ לַזְּמַן הַזֶּה.

HERE ARE SOME WORDS IN
Lesson One

אוֹמְרִים	נוֹתֵן	חָדָשׁ	שֶׁהֶחֱיָנוּ
א־מ־ר	נ־ת־ן	ח־ד־שׁ	ח־י

In each סִדוּר phrase on this page you will find at least one of these familiar words, or one that is related to it (has the same root). Practice reading these phrases. Then complete the exercises on the next page.

1   שִׁירוּ לַה׳ שִׁיר חָדָשׁ

2   אוֹר חָדָשׁ עַל צִיּוֹן תָּאִיר

3   אָבִינוּ מַלְכֵּנוּ חַדֵּשׁ עָלֵינוּ שָׁנָה טוֹבָה

4   פְּעָמִים בְּאַהֲבָה ״שְׁמַע״ אוֹמְרִים

5   וְאַל יֹאבַד יִשְׂרָאֵל, הָאוֹמְרִים ״שְׁמַע יִשְׂרָאֵל״

6   בָּרוּךְ שֶׁנָּתַן תּוֹרָה לְעַמּוֹ יִשְׂרָאֵל בִּקְדֻשָּׁתוֹ

7   בָּרוּךְ אַתָּה ה׳ נוֹתֵן הַתּוֹרָה

8   יִגְדַּל אֱלֹהִים חַי וְיִשְׁתַּבַּח

9   הוּא נוֹתֵן לֶחֶם לְכָל בָּשָׂר

10   בָּרוּךְ אַתָּה ה׳ אֱלֹהֵינוּ מֶלֶךְ הָעוֹלָם

שֶׁהֶחֱיָנוּ וְקִיְּמָנוּ וְהִגִּיעָנוּ לַזְּמַן הַזֶּה

1 Circle the familiar or related word in each phrase on the opposite page.

2 When do we say סִדוּר phrase #3? ______________________________

Which two Hebrew words gave you the answer? __________ __________

3 Write two phrases we recite when called to the תּוֹרָה.

____

____

What ''clue'' word helped you find the right answer? __________

4 Give an example of when you might say the בְּרָכָה on line #10.

____

God's Name

There are many ways to write God's name.

In the Bible and in the סִדוּר it may be written יהוה, יְיָ or יָה.

In other Hebrew books, such as this Workbook, it is written ה׳.

When *we* want to write God's name, we also write ה׳ and ד׳.
No matter how it is written, we pronounce God's name אֲדוֹנָי, which means *my Lord.* Why? There are two reasons:

1. We honor God's name above all other names in the world. We treat God's name with respect.

2. We are not really sure how to pronounce God's name. The name יהוה appears in the Bible. It is an ancient name that has been handed down to us from generation to generation, for more than 3,000 years. We don't know how to pronounce it because we have never heard it said aloud. We only read it with our eyes.

In ancient times, when there was a Temple in Jerusalem with priests who led the services, God's name יהוה was very holy. It was pronounced only on יוֹם כִּפּוּר, the holiest day in the year, when the High Priest went into the Holy of Holies of the Temple, to pray for the people of Israel.

When we *talk* about God, sometimes we don't say אֲדוֹנָי. We say אֱלֹהִים which means *God.* Some people say הַשֵּׁם, which means *the Name.* We are very careful about using God's name at all times.

CHALLENGE QUESTION
Why do you think so many ח־י words appear in the סְדוּר?

עֵץ חַיִּים

The תּוֹרָה is called עֵץ חַיִּים a *tree of life*. Here is the תְּפִלָּה we recite and sing just before we put the תּוֹרָה back into the Holy Ark, אֲרוֹן הַקּוֹדֶשׁ. Practice reading this תְּפִלָּה. If you know the melody for the last four lines, sing them.

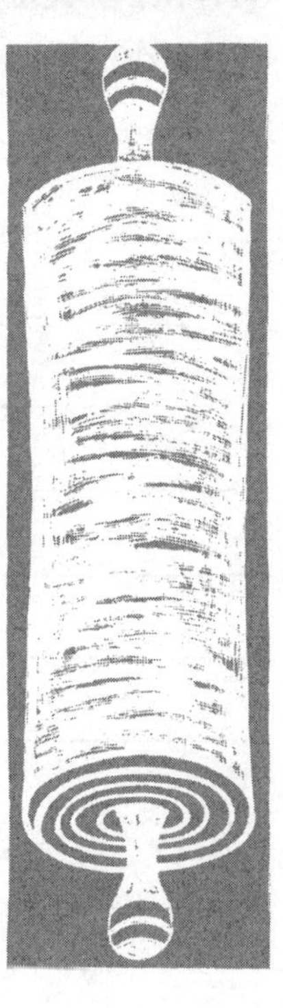

1 וּבְנֻחֹה יֹאמַר: שׁוּבָה יְיָ רִבְבוֹת אַלְפֵי יִשְׂרָאֵל.

2 קוּמָה יְיָ לִמְנוּחָתֶךָ, אַתָּה וַאֲרוֹן עֻזֶּךָ.

3 כֹּהֲנֶיךָ יִלְבְּשׁוּ צֶדֶק, וַחֲסִידֶיךָ יְרַנֵּנוּ.

4 בַּעֲבוּר דָּוִד עַבְדֶּךָ, אַל תָּשֵׁב פְּנֵי מְשִׁיחֶךָ.

5 כִּי לֶקַח טוֹב נָתַתִּי לָכֶם.

6 תּוֹרָתִי אַל תַּעֲזֹבוּ.

7 עֵץ חַיִּים הִיא לַמַּחֲזִיקִים בָּהּ.

8 וְתֹמְכֶיהָ מְאֻשָּׁר.

9 דְּרָכֶיהָ דַרְכֵי נֹעַם. וְכָל נְתִיבוֹתֶיהָ שָׁלוֹם.

10 הֲשִׁיבֵנוּ יְיָ אֵלֶיךָ וְנָשׁוּבָה, חַדֵּשׁ יָמֵינוּ כְּקֶדֶם.

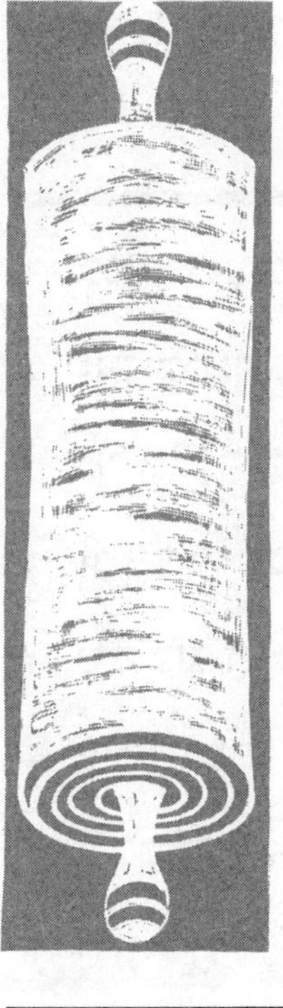

1 And when the ark rested, Moses said: Return, O Lord, to the multitude of the families of Israel.
2 Arise, O Lord, return to your sanctuary,
You and the Ark of Your glory.
3 Let Your priests be robed in righteousness, and let Your faithful sing for joy.
4 Be gracious to David, Your faithful; do not reject Your anointed.

5 I have given you good teaching.

6 Do not forsake My Torah.

7 It is a tree of life to them that hold fast to it,

8 And everyone that upholds it is happy.

9 Its ways are ways of pleasantness, and all its paths are peace.

10 Turn us to You, O Lord, and we shall return; renew our days as of old.

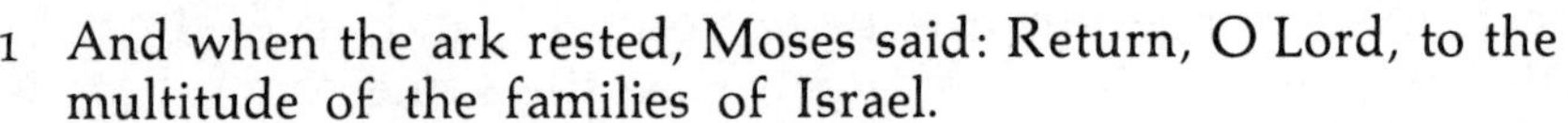

1 Copy the line in which the תּוֹרָה is called a *tree of life.*

2 Why do you think the תּוֹרָה is called a *tree of life?*

HERE ARE SOME WORDS IN
Lesson Two

אוֹכְלִים יִהְיֶה זְמַן כְּמוֹ
א־כ־ל ה־י־ה

In each סִדוּר phrase on this page you will find at least one of these familiar words, or one that is related to it (has the same root). Practice reading these phrases. Then complete the exercises on the next page.

1 כְּמוֹ שֶׁאָמְרוּ אֲבוֹתֵינוּ

2 אֵין כָּמוֹךָ בָאֱלֹהִים ה׳, וְאֵין כְּמַעֲשֶׂיךָ

3 מִי כָמוֹךָ בַּעַל גְבוּרוֹת

4 זְמַן חֵרוּתֵנוּ מִקְרָא קֹדֶשׁ זֵכֶר לִיצִיאַת מִצְרָיִם

5 יוֹם חַג הַשָּׁבֻעוֹת הַזֶּה, זְמַן מַתַּן תּוֹרָתֵנוּ

6 עַל הַנִּסִּים...שֶׁעָשִׂיתָ לַאֲבוֹתֵינוּ בַּיָּמִים הָהֵם בַּזְּמַן הַזֶּה

7 בַּיּוֹם הַהוּא יִהְיֶה ה׳ אֶחָד, וּשְׁמוֹ אֶחָד

8 וְהוּא הָיָה וְהוּא הֹוֶה וְהוּא יִהְיֶה לְתִפְאָרָה

9 שֶׁבְּכָל הַלֵּילוֹת אָנוּ אוֹכְלִין חָמֵץ וּמַצָּה, הַלַּיְלָה הַזֶּה כֻּלוֹ מַצָּה

10 בָּרוּךְ אַתָּה ה׳ אֱלֹהֵינוּ מֶלֶךְ הָעוֹלָם

שֶׁעָשָׂה נִסִּים לַאֲבוֹתֵינוּ בַּיָּמִים הָהֵם בַּזְּמַן הַזֶּה.

1 Circle the familiar or related words(s) in each phrase on the opposite page.

2 The words בַּיָּמִים הָהֵם בַּזְּמַן הַזֶּה mean *in those days at this time of the year.*

That is a ''shorthand'' way of saying ________________________________

________________________________ (Use your own words).

3 Find two phrases that include the words בַּיָּמִים הָהֵם בַּזְּמַן הַזֶּה. They are

#______ and #______. These are parts of בְּרָכוֹת said on חֲנֻכָּה and on פּוּרִים. They remind us of the נִסִּים, the *miracles*, that occurred at those times.

4 Write the words from the בְּרָכָה on line #10 that mean ''who did miracles in those days at this time''

____

How much do you know?

Read these four phrases.

שֶׁבְּכָל הַלֵּילוֹת אָנוּ אוֹכְלִין חָמֵץ וּמַצָּה 1

הַלַּיְלָה הַזֶּה כֻּלּוֹ מַצָּה.

שֶׁבְּכָל הַלֵּילוֹת אָנוּ אוֹכְלִין שְׁאָר יְרָקוֹת 2

הַלַּיְלָה הַזֶּה מָרוֹר.

שֶׁבְּכָל הַלֵּילוֹת אֵין אָנוּ מַטְבִּילִין אֲפִילוּ פַּעַם אֶחָת 3

הַלַּיְלָה הַזֶּה שְׁתֵּי פְעָמִים.

שֶׁבְּכָל הַלֵּילוֹת אָנוּ אוֹכְלִין בֵּין יוֹשְׁבִין וּבֵין מְסֻבִּין 4

הַלַּיְלָה הַזֶּה כֻּלָּנוּ מְסֻבִּין.

1 Write the Hebrew name of the holiday on which we sing

these words. ___________________

2 What is the name of the book in which these phrases

are found? ___________________

3 Write the two things that we eat on this holiday.(You will find the answer
in the phrases.)

___________________   ___________________

4 The last phrase tells us *how* we eat at this holiday meal. Describe *how* we
are to sit at the table.

____

Do you know the reason why? ___________________

____

A special kind of prayer

A בְּרָכָה is a special kind of תְּפִלָּה. It is a תְּפִלָּה that praises and thanks God for something.

Here is a בְּרָכָה that is often recited at home:

בָּרוּךְ אַתָּה ה׳ אֱלֹהֵינוּ מֶלֶךְ הָעוֹלָם הַמוֹצִיא לֶחֶם מִן הָאָרֶץ.

You are blessed, Lord our God, who brings forth bread from the earth.

We call this important בְּרָכָה — הַמוֹצִיא — and we recite it before we begin to eat a meal.

Copy the four Hebrew words that mean "who brings forth bread from the earth": _______________

Here is another בְּרָכָה for food:

בָּרוּךְ אַתָּה ה׳ אֱלֹהֵינוּ מֶלֶךְ הָעוֹלָם בּוֹרֵא מִינֵי מְזוֹנוֹת.

You are blessed, Lord our God, who creates many kinds of food.

We say this בְּרָכָה before we eat foods that are made from grains that are not bread (rye, oats, wheat, barley).

Copy the three Hebrew words that mean "who creates many kinds of food": _______________

Turn to page 14 in your textbook. Which בְּרָכָה did the children recite?

בִּרְכַּת הַמָּזוֹן

Did you ever think about how much effort goes into preparing a meal? Someone must cook and serve it. Someone must shop for the food. Many people have planted, grown and harvested the food we buy. But above all, God created the raw materials that become our food. That is why we begin a meal with the בְּרָכָה: בָּרוּךְ אַתָּה ה' אֱלֹהֵינוּ מֶלֶךְ הָעוֹלָם הַמּוֹצִיא לֶחֶם מִן הָאָרֶץ. And that is why we end the meal with בִּרְכַּת הַמָּזוֹן.

1 בָּרוּךְ אַתָּה יְיָ, אֱלֹהֵינוּ מֶלֶךְ הָעוֹלָם,

2 הַזָּן אֶת הָעוֹלָם כֻּלּוֹ בְּטוּבוֹ,

3 בְּחֵן בְּחֶסֶד וּבְרַחֲמִים.

4 הוּא נוֹתֵן לֶחֶם לְכָל בָּשָׂר, כִּי לְעוֹלָם חַסְדּוֹ.

5 וּבְטוּבוֹ הַגָּדוֹל תָּמִיד לֹא חָסַר לָנוּ,

6 וְאַל יֶחְסַר לָנוּ מָזוֹן לְעוֹלָם וָעֶד בַּעֲבוּר שְׁמוֹ הַגָּדוֹל

7 כִּי הוּא אֵל זָן וּמְפַרְנֵס לַכֹּל,

8 וּמֵטִיב לַכֹּל, וּמֵכִין מָזוֹן לְכָל בְּרִיּוֹתָיו אֲשֶׁר בָּרָא.

9 בָּרוּךְ אַתָּה יְיָ, הַזָּן אֶת הַכֹּל.

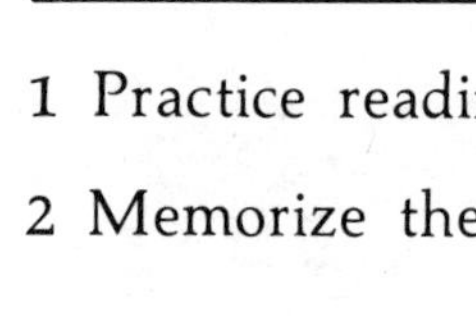

1 Blessed are You, Lord our God, King of the world,

2 Who feeds the entire world with goodness,

3 With grace, with kindness and with mercy.

4 You give food to all people, for Your kindness lasts forever.

5 Because of Your great goodness we have never lacked food;

6 May it never fail us, because of Your great name

7 For You support and assist all creatures,

8 And provide food for all You have created.

9 Blessed are You, O Lord, who gives food to everyone.

1 Practice reading בִּרְכַּת הַמָזוֹן.

2 Memorize the last line in Hebrew and in English.

HERE ARE SOME WORDS IN
Lesson Three

פְּרִי   גָּדוֹל   תְּפִלּוֹת   כִּי
ג־ד־ל

In each סִדּוּר phrase on this page you will find at least one of these familiar words, or one that is related to it (has the same root). Practice reading these phrases. Then complete the exercises on the next page.

1   כִּי בָנוּ בָחַרְתָּ וְאוֹתָנוּ קִדַּשְׁתָּ

2   כִּי מִצִּיּוֹן תֵּצֵא תוֹרָה וּדְבַר ה׳ מִירוּשָׁלַיִם

3   הָאֵל הַמֶּלֶךְ, הַגָּדוֹל וְהַקָּדוֹשׁ בַּשָּׁמַיִם וּבָאָרֶץ

4   כִּי אַתָּה שׁוֹמֵעַ תְּפִלּוֹת עַמְּךָ יִשְׂרָאֵל בְּרַחֲמִים

5   בָּרוּךְ אַתָּה ה׳, שׁוֹמֵעַ תְּפִלָּה

6   רְצֵה ה׳ אֱלֹהֵינוּ בְּעַמְּךָ יִשְׂרָאֵל וּבִתְפִלָּתָם

7   וּתְפִלָּתָם בְּאַהֲבָה תְקַבֵּל בְּרָצוֹן

8   גָּדוֹל ה׳ וּמְהֻלָּל מְאֹד וְלִגְדֻלָּתוֹ אֵין חֵקֶר

9   בָּרוּךְ אַתָּה ה׳ אֱלֹהֵינוּ מֶלֶךְ הָעוֹלָם בּוֹרֵא פְּרִי הַגָּפֶן.

10   בָּרוּךְ אַתָּה ה׳ אֱלֹהֵינוּ מֶלֶךְ הָעוֹלָם בּוֹרֵא פְּרִי הָעֵץ.

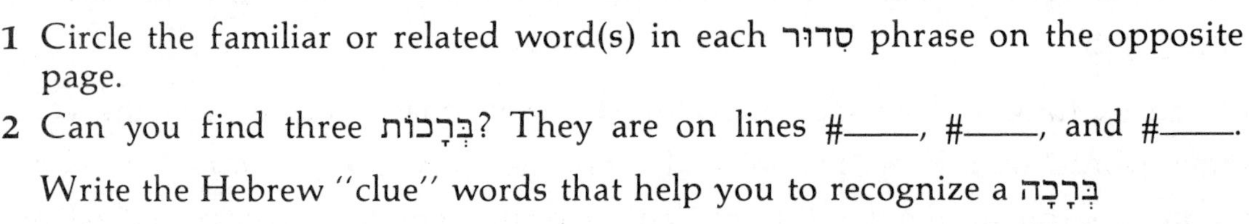

1 Circle the familiar or related word(s) in each סִדוּר phrase on the opposite page.

2 Can you find three בְּרָכוֹת? They are on lines #____, #____, and #____. Write the Hebrew "clue" words that help you to recognize a בְּרָכָה

____

3 Complete this English sentence: The Siddur contains __________ and __________. (You will find the answer in the textbook, on page 24.)

4 Complete this Hebrew sentence: __________ וּ __________ בַּסִדוּר יֵשׁ

Who wrote the תְּפִלוֹת in the סִדוּר?

Here is part of the תְּפִלָה that King Solomon composed when he dedicated the great Temple he built in Jerusalem:

הֹ' אֱלֹהֵי יִשְׂרָאֵל, אֵין כָּמוֹךָ אֱלֹהִים בַּשָׁמַיִם מִמַּעַל וּבָאָרֶץ מִתַּחַת.

O Lord, God of Israel, there is no god like You in the heavens above, and on the earth below.

King Solomon's father, King David, had composed a similar תְּפִלָה.

אֵין כָּמוֹךָ בָאֱלֹהִים ה', וְאֵין כְּמַעֲשֶׂיךָ.

There is none like You among the gods, O Lord, and there are no deeds like Yours.

We recite King David's תְּפִלָה each time we take the תוֹרָה out to read in בֵּית הַכְּנֶסֶת.

It's an exciting and wonderful feeling to know that today we say the very same words that King David said, and the very same words that King Solomon wrote on the day that he dedicated the Temple in ancient Jerusalem.

CHALLENGE QUESTIONS

1 Read the תְּפִלוֹת recited by King Solomon and King David.

Write the English words that are almost the same in each תְּפִלָה.

King Solomon: There is _______________________________

King David: There is _______________________________

2 What do Solomon's and David's prayers tell us about God?

____

All kinds of prayers

The סִדוּר is a collection or *arrangement*, סֵדֶר, of תְּפִלוֹת.

Some of the תְּפִלוֹת give thanks to God.

Some of the תְּפִלוֹת praise God.

Some of the תְּפִלוֹת ask God to help us.

Some of the תְּפִלוֹת remind us of the wonderful world in which we live, and of the Creator of that world.

Here is a תְּפִלָה in which we thank God:

מוֹדֶה אֲנִי לְפָנֶיךָ, מֶלֶךְ חַי וְקַיָּם, שֶׁהֶחֱזַרְתָּ בִּי נִשְׁמָתִי בְּחֶמְלָה, רַבָּה אֱמוּנָתֶךָ.

I give thanks to You, living and enduring King, for having returned my soul to me with compassion. Your trust is great.

1 Write a Hebrew word that you know that means *thank you.* ________________

2 Find a word in this תְּפִלָה that means *I thank you.* ________________

3 When would be a good time to say this תְּפִלָה?

____

אֵין כָּמוֹךָ

Here is the תְּפִלָּה we sing when we take the תּוֹרָה out of the אֲרוֹן קוֹדֶשׁ, the Holy Ark. Practice reading the prayer. Then, if you know the melody—sing it.

1 אֵין כָּמוֹךָ בָאֱלֹהִים, אֲדֹנָי, וְאֵין כְּמַעֲשֶׂיךָ.

2 מַלְכוּתְךָ מַלְכוּת כָּל עֹלָמִים, וּמֶמְשַׁלְתְּךָ בְּכָל דֹר נָדֹר.

3 ה׳ מֶלֶךְ, ה׳ מָלָךְ, ה׳ יִמְלֹךְ לְעֹלָם וָעֶד.

4 ה׳ עֹז לְעַמּוֹ יִתֵּן, ה׳ יְבָרֵךְ אֶת עַמּוֹ בַשָּׁלוֹם.

5 אַב הָרַחֲמִים, הֵיטִיבָה בִרְצוֹנְךָ אֶת צִיּוֹן,

6 תִּבְנֶה חוֹמוֹת יְרוּשָׁלָיִם.

7 כִּי בְךָ לְבַד בָּטָחְנוּ,

8 מֶלֶךְ אֵל רָם וְנִשָּׂא, אֲדוֹן עוֹלָמִים.

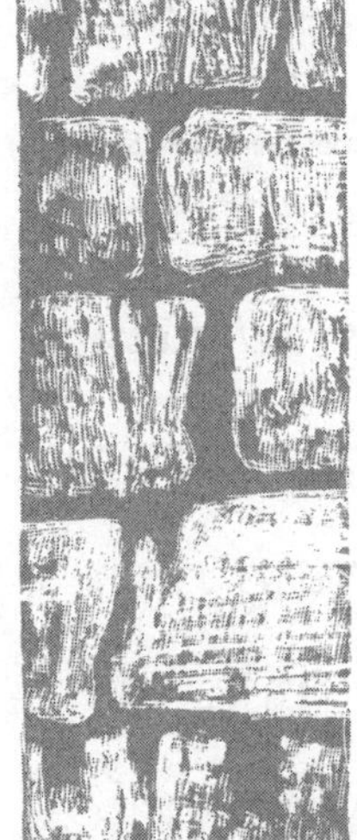

1 There is none like You, Lord, among the mighty;
  and no works are like Yours.

2 Your kingdom is an everlasting kingdom,
  and Your dominion endures throughout all generations.

3 The Lord is King; the Lord was King;
  the Lord will be King forever and ever.

4 The Lord will give strength to His people;
  He will bless His people with peace.

5 Merciful Father, deal kindly with Zion.

6 Rebuild the walls of Jerusalem.

7 In You alone we put our trust.

8 Exalted God and King, Lord of the universe.

Copy the line that is the same תְּפִלָה written by King David. (See page 20 of this Workbook.)

Compare the English translation on this page with the English translation on p. 20.

Are the *English words* the same? ___________

Is the *idea* of the תְּפִלָה the same? ___________

Write the idea expressed in this line, using your own words.

HERE ARE SOME WORDS IN
Lesson Four

בּוֹרֵא   אַחֲרֵי   לִפְנֵי   עֵץ   אֲדָמָה
בּ־ר־א

In each סִדוּר phrase on this page you will find at least one of these familiar words, or one that is related to it (has the same root). Practice reading these phrases. Then complete the exercises on the next page.

1   יוֹצֵר אוֹר וּבוֹרֵא חֹשֶׁךְ

2   עֹשֶׂה שָׁלוֹם וּבוֹרֵא אֶת הַכֹּל

3   וְאַחֲרֵי כִּכְלוֹת הַכֹּל לְבַדוֹ יִמְלֹךְ נוֹרָא

4   וְזֹאת הַתּוֹרָה אֲשֶׁר שָׂם מֹשֶׁה לִפְנֵי בְּנֵי יִשְׂרָאֵל

5   וְתֵן בְּרָכָה עַל פְּנֵי הָאֲדָמָה

6   לִפְנֵי מֶלֶךְ מַלְכֵי הַמְּלָכִים, הַקָּדוֹש בָּרוּךְ הוּא

7   עֵץ חַיִּים הִיא לַמַּחֲזִיקִים בָּה

8   בּוֹרֵא יוֹם וָלַיְלָה...וּמַבְדִּיל בֵּין יוֹם וּבֵין לַיְלָה

9   בָּרוּךְ אַתָּה ה׳ אֱלֹהֵינוּ מֶלֶךְ הָעוֹלָם בּוֹרֵא יוֹם וָלָיְלָה

10   בָּרוּךְ אַתָּה ה׳ אֱלֹהֵינוּ מֶלֶךְ הָעוֹלָם בּוֹרֵא פְּרִי הָאֲדָמָה

1 Find five phrases on the opposite page that tell about God the Creator.

#_______ #_______ #_______ #_______ #_______

Which word means *create?* _______

2 Phrase #2 describes God doing and creating two things. What are they?

_____________ _____________

Do you know what they mean? _____________ _____________.

3 Phrase #10 describes God creating_______________________________

4 Phrases #8 and #9 describe God creating _____________ and _____________.
(If you don't know the second word, try to *guess* its meaning.)

Every person is created in the image of God

The word אֲדָמָה means ___________________.

Which word in the phrase כִּי בְּצֶלֶם אֱלֹהִים נִבְרָא הָאָדָם is related to אֲדָמָה?

___________________.

The word אָדָם means *person, human being.* It is also a proper name. Who

was the person named אָדָם? ________________

Why do you think this was his name? ______________

(If you are not sure, you can look in the Bible to find out. The answer is in the Book of Genesis, chapter 2, verse 7.

The word בּוֹרֵא means ___________ . What is its root? _________

Which word in the phrase כִּי בְּצֶלֶם אֱלֹהִים נִבְרָא הָאָדָם has the same three-

letter root? __________

When we see Hebrew words with the same root, we know that

____

צֶלֶם is a very old Hebrew word found in the Bible. You can find it in the Book of Genesis, chapter 1, verse 27.

What does צֶלֶם mean? _________ (You know all the other words in the Hebrew phrase כִּי בְּצֶלֶם אֱלֹהִים נִבְרָא הָאָדָם — so you can figure out what צֶלֶם

means!) ____________

Our תְּפִלּוֹת describe God as גָּדוֹל and טוֹב. We know that a person can be גָּדוֹל and טוֹב, too. But we also know that this is not always the case. A person can *try* to be great — to do a difficult job — to take on an important responsibility. A person can *choose* or *learn* to be good — to think of others, and be helpful. But a person can also choose to be small and selfish, thoughtless or dishonest.

It is not easy, but every person can try to copy the qualities that are part of God. That is why we say that every person is created in the image of God.

כִּי בְּצֶלֶם אֱלֹהִים נִבְרָא הָאָדָם

CHALLENGE QUESTIONS

1 How can every person try to copy the qualities of God? Give examples.

____

____

2 What happens when we ignore these goals? _______________________

____

3 Complete this sentence: When we try to copy God's qualities in our own lives, the world _______________________

____

Learning about God

Here are parts of prayers that tell us about God.

1 הָאֵל הַמֶּלֶךְ הַגָּדוֹל וְהַקָּדוֹשׁ בַּשָּׁמַיִם וּבָאָרֶץ

2 הָאֵל הַגָּדוֹל הַגִּבּוֹר וְהַנּוֹרָא, אֵל עֶלְיוֹן

3 כִּי לְךָ ה׳ הַגְּדוּלָה וְהַגְּבוּרָה וְהַתִּפְאֶרֶת

4 גָּדְלוֹ וְטוּבוֹ מָלֵא עוֹלָם

5 גָּדוֹל ה׳ וּמְהֻלָּל מְאֹד, וְלִגְדֻלָּתוֹ אֵין חֵקֶר

6 טוֹב ה׳ לַכֹּל וְרַחֲמָיו עַל כָּל מַעֲשָׂיו

1 You know a Hebrew word that means *big, large*. Write it here. _________

This word also means *great*.

If you take out the ו sound, what Hebrew letters are left? ___ ___ ___

In every line but two, above, you will find a word that belongs to the same
___ ___ ___ family. Circle each word.

2 Now that you know another meaning for this word-family, you can
complete this sentence: God is _______________.

3 Which lines above do not include any word from this family? #___ #____

CHALLENGE QUESTION

4 Describe *how* you feel when you are reminded that God is _______ and
________, and *why* you feel that way.

____

____

____

The סִדּוּר and the תּוֹרָה teach us about God. The very first sentence in the first book of the תּוֹרָה tells us something special about God. Here is the sentence:

בְּרֵאשִׁית בָּרָא אֱלֹהִים אֵת הַשָּׁמַיִם וְאֵת הָאָרֶץ

In the beginning, God created the heavens and the earth...

In the סִדּוּר we read that each day God, in His goodness, renews His work of creation.

וּבְטוּבוֹ מְחַדֵּשׁ בְּכָל יוֹם תָּמִיד מַעֲשֵׂה בְרֵאשִׁית

These בְּרָכוֹת praise and thank God the Creator.

בָּרוּךְ אַתָּה ה׳ אֱלֹהֵינוּ מֶלֶךְ הָעוֹלָם בּוֹרֵא פְּרִי הָעֵץ.

You are blessed, Lord our God, King of the world, who creates the fruit of the tree.

בָּרוּךְ אַתָּה ה׳ אֱלֹהֵינוּ מֶלֶךְ הָעוֹלָם בּוֹרֵא פְּרִי הָאֲדָמָה.

You are blessed, Lord our God, King of the world, who creates the fruit of the ground.

בָּרוּךְ אַתָּה ה׳ אֱלֹהֵינוּ מֶלֶךְ הָעוֹלָם בּוֹרֵא פְּרִי הַגָּפֶן.

You are blessed, Lord our God, King of the world, who creates the fruit of the vine (wine).

1 Which Hebrew word in each of these בְּרָכוֹת reminds us that God is the Creator? _________

הַמַּעֲרִיב עֲרָבִים

Here is a תְּפִלָה that we recite in the Evening Service. It praises God for some of the things He has created. Practice reading this תְּפִלָה.

1 בָּרוּךְ אַתָּה יְיָ, אֱלֹהֵינוּ מֶלֶךְ הָעוֹלָם

2 אֲשֶׁר בִּדְבָרוֹ מַעֲרִיב עֲרָבִים.

3 בְּחָכְמָה פּוֹתֵחַ שְׁעָרִים, וּבִתְבוּנָה מְשַׁנֶּה עִתִּים,

4 וּמַחֲלִיף אֶת הַזְּמַנִּים,

5 וּמְסַדֵּר אֶת הַכּוֹכָבִים בְּמִשְׁמְרוֹתֵיהֶם בָּרָקִיעַ כִּרְצוֹנוֹ.

6 בּוֹרֵא יוֹם וָלַיְלָה, גּוֹלֵל אוֹר מִפְּנֵי חֹשֶׁךְ וְחֹשֶׁךְ מִפְּנֵי אוֹר,

7 וּמַעֲבִיר יוֹם וּמֵבִיא לַיְלָה, וּמַבְדִּיל בֵּין יוֹם וּבֵין לָיְלָה,

8 יְיָ צְבָאוֹת שְׁמוֹ.

9 אֵל חַי וְקַיָּם תָּמִיד יִמְלֹךְ עָלֵינוּ לְעוֹלָם וָעֶד.

10 בָּרוּךְ אַתָּה יְיָ, הַמַּעֲרִיב עֲרָבִים.

1 Praised are You Lord our God, King of the universe.

2 In wisdom You bring on the evening twilight and open the gates of the heavens to usher in a new day.

3 In understanding You arrange the changes of time

4 And the succession of seasons.

5 You set the stars in their courses in the day, according to Your will.

6 You create day and night, rolling away the light before the darkness and the darkness before the light.

7 You make the day fade into the night and set a boundary between day and night.

8 You are the Lord of all the heavenly hosts.

9 O everliving God, as You rule over the kingdom of nature, may You also rule over us forever and ever.

10 Praised are You, O Lord, who brings on the evening twilight.

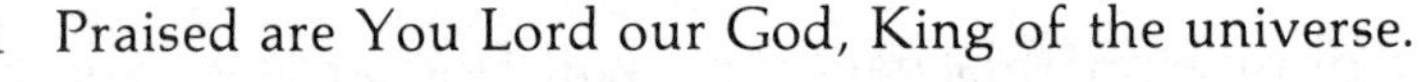

1 The first and last lines of this תְּפִלָּה are בְּרָכוֹת. What are the clue words that tell you this?

2 Think about these two בְּרָכוֹת. What do they praise God for?

HERE ARE SOME WORDS IN
Lesson Five

לָנוּ	אֱלֹהֵינוּ	עוֹלָם	בָּרוּךְ	אֶרֶץ
			בּ־ר־ךְ	

In each סִדוּר phrase on this page you will find at least one of these familiar words, or one that is related to it (has the same root). Practice reading these phrases. Then complete the exercises on the next page.

1 אֵין לָנוּ מֶלֶךְ אֶלָּא אַתָּה

2 בָּרְכוּ אֶת ה׳ הַמְבֹרָךְ

3 בָּרוּךְ ה׳ הַמְבֹרָךְ לְעוֹלָם וָעֶד

4 בָּרוּךְ אַתָּה ה׳ עַל הָאָרֶץ וְעַל הַמָּזוֹן

5 בָּרוּךְ אַתָּה ה׳ אֱלֹהֵינוּ מֶלֶךְ הָעוֹלָם אֲשֶׁר נָתַן לָנוּ תּוֹרַת אֱמֶת

6 וַאֲנַחְנוּ נְבָרֵךְ יָהּ מֵעַתָּה וְעַד עוֹלָם

7 כִּי ה׳ הוּא הָאֱלֹהִים בַּשָּׁמַיִם מִמַּעַל וְעַל הָאָרֶץ מִתַּחַת

8 הָאֵל הַמֶּלֶךְ הַגָּדוֹל וְהַקָּדוֹשׁ בַּשָּׁמַיִם וּבָאָרֶץ

9 קָדוֹשׁ קָדוֹשׁ קָדוֹשׁ ה׳ צְבָאוֹת, מְלֹא כָל הָאָרֶץ כְּבוֹדוֹ

10 בָּרוּךְ אַתָּה ה׳ אֱלֹהֵינוּ מֶלֶךְ הָעוֹלָם הַמּוֹצִיא לֶחֶם מִן הָאָרֶץ.

1 Find two בְּרָכוֹת on the opposite page that include the Hebrew word for *our God.* Copy the two בְּרָכוֹת.

____

____

2 Find six phrases that include a word in the ב־ר־ך family. Circle the words you find. (Careful! Some phrases may have more than one ב־ר־ך word.) What meaning do all these words share? _______________________

3 You have learned that עוֹלָם means _______________. Sometimes it can also mean *forever.* In phrases #3 and #6, the word עוֹלָם means *forever.* See if you can write the meaning of each phrase.

#3 ____

#6 ____

Showing respect for God's name

Because the name of God appears very frequently in the תְּפִלּוֹת and בְּרָכוֹת in the סִדּוּר, we treat the סִדּוּר with special respect.

If we are interrupted while we are reading, we don't turn down the corner of the page. We put a book-mark between the pages. When we are finished reading, we don't leave the סִדּוּר lying around, but put it away. Some people kiss the סִדּוּר as a sign of respect.

To what other object that has God's name written in it do we show special respect? (Write it in Hebrew). _______________________

____

When we show respect for God's name, we are showing respect for God.

Can you think of other ways to show our respect for God when we are in בֵּית כְּנֶסֶת? (Think of how we look, what we do, how we sound.)

____

____

Do you remember what the phrase כִּי בְּצֶלֶם אֱלֹהִים נִבְרָא הָאָדָם means? You learned the phrase on page 26.
Write the meaning here.

____

____

When we show respect for other people, we are also showing respect for God. Here are four possible situations:

_____ (a) David's class was taking a test under the honor system. Saul wanted to copy from David's paper. David said no because the teacher trusted them to be honest.

_____ (b) Sharon gave the little boy next door, who is mentally retarded, a ride on her bicycle.

_____ (c) Amy telephoned her friend Susan and complained, "My mother is so mean. She won't let me see you tomorrow because my grandfather is coming over to visit."

_____ (d) While rounding third base, Eric knocked Steven down. Steven cut his lip and ran home crying. Eric felt bad but he thought: "After all, it was just an accident, I didn't mean to do it."

Rate each situation from 1 to 4 as follows:

1 - an important way to show respect for God

2 - a good way to show respect for God

3 - not an important way to show respect for God

4 - no way to show respect for God

CHALLENGE QUESTION

In the situations you rated 3 and 4, how could the people involved have shown more respect for God? _____________________

____

My God — Our God

The תְּפִלּוֹת in the סִדוּר contain many names for God. We already know ה׳ and יְיָ. We also know אֵל and אֱלֹהִים.

אֱלֹהִים can be combined with many word-endings (suffixes) to form these new words.

our God	אֱלֹהֵינוּ	God	אֵל
(his) its God	אֱלֹהָיו	God	אֱלֹהִים
my God	אֱלֹהַי	God of	אֱלֹהֵי

Read these Hebrew phrases and fill in the missing words in the English translation on the next page.

1. אֵל אָדוֹן עַל כָּל הַמַּעֲשִׂים

2. הָאֵל הַגָּדוֹל הַגִּבּוֹר וְהַנּוֹרָא

3. אֲרוֹמִמְךָ אֱלֹהַי הַמֶּלֶךְ

4. אַשְׁרֵי הָעָם שֶׁה׳ אֱלֹהָיו

5. אַתָּה הוּא אֱלֹהֵינוּ

6. שְׁמַע יִשְׂרָאֵל ה׳ אֱלֹהֵינוּ ה׳ אֶחָד

7. בָּרוּךְ אַתָּה ה׳ אֱלֹהֵינוּ וֵאלֹהֵי אֲבוֹתֵינוּ

8. אֱלֹהֵי אַבְרָהָם, אֱלֹהֵי יִצְחָק וֵאלֹהֵי יַעֲקֹב

1 אֱלֹהֵינוּ means _________ _________. When we say אֱלֹהֵינוּ, who is the *we* that

is talking? ___________________________________

2 In phrase #7, who are אֲבוֹתֵינוּ, *our fathers*? ___________________________
Find another phrase that gives the answer. Write the answer in Hebrew.

____

____

3 If you wanted to say *my God*, in Hebrew, you would say __________ .

If you wanted to say *our God* in Hebrew, you would say __________ .

1 _________, Lord of all that is done

2 The great, strong, and awesome _________

3 I will raise You high, _________ _________ the King

4 Happy is the people that has the Lord as _________ _________

5 You are _________ _________

6 Hear O Israel, the Lord _________ _________, the Lord is One

7 You are praised, Lord, _________ _________ and _________ _________ our fathers
(ancestors)

8 _________ _________ Abraham, _________ _________ Isaac, and _________ _________
Jacob

אֲדוֹן עוֹלָם

God rules over all the world. Because God is great, good and powerful, we trust that He will protect us. That is why we sing אֲדוֹן עוֹלָם.

1 אֲדוֹן עוֹלָם אֲשֶׁר מָלַךְ   בְּטֶרֶם כָּל יְצִיר נִבְרָא.

2 לְעֵת נַעֲשָׂה בְחֶפְצוֹ כֹּל   אֲזַי מֶלֶךְ שְׁמוֹ נִקְרָא.

3 וְאַחֲרֵי כִּכְלוֹת הַכֹּל   לְבַדּוֹ יִמְלֹךְ נוֹרָא.

4 וְהוּא הָיָה וְהוּא הֹוֶה   וְהוּא יִהְיֶה בְּתִפְאָרָה.

5 וְהוּא אֶחָד וְאֵין שֵׁנִי   לְהַמְשִׁיל לוֹ לְהַחְבִּירָה.

6 בְּלִי רֵאשִׁית בְּלִי תַכְלִית   וְלוֹ הָעֹז וְהַמִּשְׂרָה.

7 וְהוּא אֵלִי וְחַי גֹּאֲלִי   וְצוּר חֶבְלִי בְּעֵת צָרָה.

8 וְהוּא נִסִּי וּמָנוֹס לִי   מְנָת כּוֹסִי בְּיוֹם אֶקְרָא.

9 בְּיָדוֹ אַפְקִיד רוּחִי   בְּעֵת אִישַׁן וְאָעִירָה.

10 וְעִם רוּחִי גְּוִיָּתִי   יְיָ לִי וְלֹא אִירָא.

1 The Lord Eternal reigned supreme
   When all the world was naught,
2 His name is praised by every life
   His gracious will has wrought.
3 And if this world should ever cease,
   He still will reign in awe,
4 The tides of time will not erase
   The splendor of His Law.
5 In oneness and infinity
   He is beyond compare,
6 The glory of His sovereign might
   Is written everywhere.
7 He is my Rock, my Refuge sure,
   My help when grief assails,
8 My cup of life He maketh full,
   His mercy never fails.
9 My life is ever in His hand,
   With Him there is no fear,
10 When I sleep and when I wake
   I know that He is near.

1 Copy the Hebrew line that tells us that God is the Lord of the world, who ruled even before anything was created.

2 Read the last four lines of the English translation. Have you ever felt that God was near? Write about this feeling from your own experience if you can.

HERE ARE SOME WORDS IN
Lesson Six

מוֹצִיאָה	יוֹשְׁבִים מִינֵי	מִן	יוֹשְׁבִים	שָׂמֵחַ
			יָ־שָׁ־ב	שָׂ־מָ־ח

In each סִדּוּר phrase on this page you will find at least one of these familiar words, or one that is related to it (has the same root). Practice reading these phrases. Then complete the exercises on the next page.

1 יִשְׂמַח מֹשֶׁה בְּמַתְּנַת חֶלְקוֹ

2 מִן הַמֵּצַר קָרָאתִי יָהּ עָנָנִי בַמֶּרְחָב יָהּ

3 מְנוּחָה וְשִׂמְחָה אוֹר לַיְּהוּדִים

4 בָּרוּךְ אַתָּה ה׳ אֱלֹהֵינוּ מֶלֶךְ הָעוֹלָם הַמּוֹצִיא לֶחֶם מִן הָאָרֶץ.

5 יִשְׂמְחוּ בְמַלְכוּתְךָ שׁוֹמְרֵי שַׁבָּת וְקוֹרְאֵי עֹנֶג

6 וְנִשְׂמַח בְּדִבְרֵי תוֹרָתֶךָ וּבְמִצְוֹתֶיךָ לְעוֹלָם וָעֶד

7 שֶׁבְּכָל הַלֵּילוֹת אָנוּ אוֹכְלִין בֵּין יוֹשְׁבִין וּבֵין מְסֻבִּין

8 בָּרוּךְ אַתָּה ה׳ אֱלֹהֵינוּ מֶלֶךְ הָעוֹלָם בּוֹרֵא מִינֵי מְזוֹנוֹת.

9 בָּרוּךְ אַתָּה ה׳ אֱלֹהֵינוּ מֶלֶךְ הָעוֹלָם בּוֹרֵא מִינֵי בְשָׂמִים.

10 אִלּוּ הוֹצִיאָנוּ מִמִּצְרַיִם וְלֹא עָשָׂה בָהֶם שְׁפָטִים

1 How many בְּרָכוֹת can you find on the opposite page? _______ How did you

recognize them?____

2 There are four *different* words belonging to the שׂ־מ־ח word family in the סִדּוּר phrases. List them here:

_____________ _____________ _____________ _____________

3 Write the English meaning of each of these words. Can you find the words or related words in the סִדּוּר phrases? Write the numbers of the lines on which they appear under each word.

_____ יוֹשְׁבִים _____ מִינֵי _____ מִן _____ מוֹצִיאָהּ

    line #__   line #__   line #__   line #__

    line #__   line #__   line #__

God is King

1 What are the first six words of every בְּרָכָה?

בָּרוּךְ _________ _________ _________ _________ _________

2 What is the idea expressed in these six words?

____

3 What are some of the qualities of a king or ruler?

____

____

4 Kings are generally very wealthy. What kind of gifts might a king give to

someone he loved? _______________________________

____

5 The סִדוּר tells us which gift God, the King of kings, מֶלֶךְ מַלְכֵי הַמְּלָכִים

gave us, the Jewish people.

בָּרוּךְ שֶׁנָּתַן תּוֹרָה לְעַמּוֹ יִשְׂרָאֵל בִּקְדֻשָׁתוֹ.

What was the gift? ________________________________

6 Why do you think this is a valuable gift? __________________

____

____

____

Happy songs

Read the following סִדוּר phrases and circle all the Hebrew words that belong to the שׂ-מ-ח word-family. What meaning do all these words share?

1 יִשְׂמְחוּ הַשָּׁמַיִם וְתָגֵל הָאָרֶץ

2 יִשְׂמַח מֹשֶׁה בְּמַתְּנַת חֶלְקוֹ

3 וְנִשְׂמַח בְּדִבְרֵי תוֹרָתֶךְ וּבְמִצְוֹתֶיךָ לְעוֹלָם וָעֶד

4 שְׂמֵחִים בְּצֵאתָם וְשָׂשִׂים בְּבוֹאָם

5 מְנוּחָה וְשִׂמְחָה אוֹר לַיְּהוּדִים

6 יִשְׂמְחוּ בְמַלְכוּתְךָ שׁוֹמְרֵי שַׁבָּת וְקוֹרְאֵי עֹנֶג

In each line there is one word that does not belong with the others. Cross it out. Write the word-family to which the remaining words belong, and the meaning that is shared by all those words.

meaning	word-family	
————	————	1 נוֹתְנִים נָתַן נוֹסֵעַ נוֹתֵן
————	————	2 יִשְׂמַח מָשִׁיחַ שְׂמֵחִים וְנִשְׂמַח
————	————	3 בְּרָכָה הַמְבֹרָךְ בּוֹרֵא בָּרוּךְ
————	————	4 הַגָּדוֹל יִגְדַּל לִגְדוּלָתוֹ דֶּגֶל
————	————	5 אֲדוֹנִי לָאָדוֹן אֱלֹהֵינוּ אֲדוֹנֵינוּ

A בְּרָכָה
for pleasant smells

You already know that we say בְּרָכוֹת for different things we taste. How many examples of such בְּרָכוֹת can you remember?

1 בָּרוּךְ אַתָּה ה׳ אֱלֹהֵינוּ מֶלֶךְ הָעוֹלָם _______________________

2 בָּרוּךְ אַתָּה ה׳ אֱלֹהֵינוּ _______________________

3 בָּרוּךְ אַתָּה ה׳ _______________________

_______________________ 4

_______________________ 5

Here is a בְּרָכָה to say when we smell something good.

בָּרוּךְ אַתָּה ה׳ אֱלֹהֵינוּ מֶלֶךְ הָעוֹלָם בּוֹרֵא מִינֵי בְשָׂמִים.

You are blessed, Lord our God, King of the world who creates many kinds of spices.

We recite this בְּרָכָה at the end of שַׁבָּת, during the הַבְדָלָה service. We hope that the coming week will be a pleasant and enjoyable one, and we smell sweet spices.

בְּרָכוֹת Special for special sights

When we see a rainbow in the sky, we say this בְּרָכָה.

בָּרוּךְ אַתָּה ה', אֱלֹהֵינוּ מֶלֶךְ הָעוֹלָם, זוֹכֵר הַבְּרִית, וְנֶאֱמָן בִּבְרִיתוֹ וְקַיָם בְּמַאֲמָרוֹ.

When we see lightning, or an unusual natural sight — like Niagara Falls, a stalactite-cave, a national park, etc., we say this בְּרָכָה.

בָּרוּךְ אַתָּה ה', אֱלֹהֵינוּ מֶלֶךְ הָעוֹלָם, עוֹשֶׂה מַעֲשֵׂה בְּרֵאשִׁית.

CHALLENGE QUESTIONS:

1 Why do we say ... בָּרוּךְ אַתָּה ה', אֱלֹהֵינוּ מֶלֶךְ הָעוֹלָם, זוֹכֵר הַבְּרִית when we see a rainbow? (You can find the answer in the story of Noah in the Bible; Genesis 9:8-17.)

____

____

2 Describe an unusual natural sight that you have visited or read about, for which you would say,

בָּרוּךְ אַתָּה ה', אֱלֹהֵינוּ מֶלֶךְ הָעוֹלָם, עוֹשֶׂה מַעֲשֵׂה בְּרֵאשִׁית.

____

____

3 Why don't we say a בְּרָכָה when we see a skyscraper, or a magnificent synagogue, or an Apollo rocket taking off?

____

יִשְׂמְחוּ בְּמַלְכוּתֶךָ

We recite many תְּפִלוֹת on שַׁבָּת that tell about the joy of Shabbat. The following תְּפִלָה is part of the עֲמִידָה prayer recited on שַׁבָּת. Practice reading the תְּפִלָה.

1 יִשְׂמְחוּ בְּמַלְכוּתֶךָ שׁוֹמְרֵי שַׁבָּת וְקוֹרְאֵי עֹנֶג.

2 עַם מְקַדְּשֵׁי שְׁבִיעִי כֻּלָם יִשְׂבְּעוּ וְיִתְעַנְּגוּ מִטּוּבֶךָ,

3 וּבַשְּׁבִיעִי רָצִיתָ בּוֹ וְקִדַּשְׁתּוֹ,

4 חֶמְדַּת יָמִים אוֹתוֹ קָרָאתָ זֵכֶר לְמַעֲשֵׂה בְרֵאשִׁית.

5 אֱלֹהֵינוּ וֵאלֹהֵי אֲבוֹתֵינוּ רְצֵה בִמְנוּחָתֵנוּ.

6 קַדְּשֵׁנוּ בְּמִצְוֹתֶיךָ וְתֵן חֶלְקֵנוּ בְּתוֹרָתֶךָ.

7 שַׂבְּעֵנוּ מִטּוּבֶךָ וְשַׂמְּחֵנוּ בִּישׁוּעָתֶךָ.

8 וְטַהֵר לִבֵּנוּ לְעָבְדְּךָ בֶּאֱמֶת.

9 וְהַנְחִילֵנוּ יְיָ אֱלֹהֵינוּ בְּאַהֲבָה וּבְרָצוֹן שַׁבַּת קָדְשֶׁךָ,

10 וְיָנוּחוּ בָה יִשְׂרָאֵל מְקַדְּשֵׁי שְׁמֶךָ.

11 בָּרוּךְ אַתָּה יְיָ מְקַדֵּשׁ הַשַּׁבָּת.

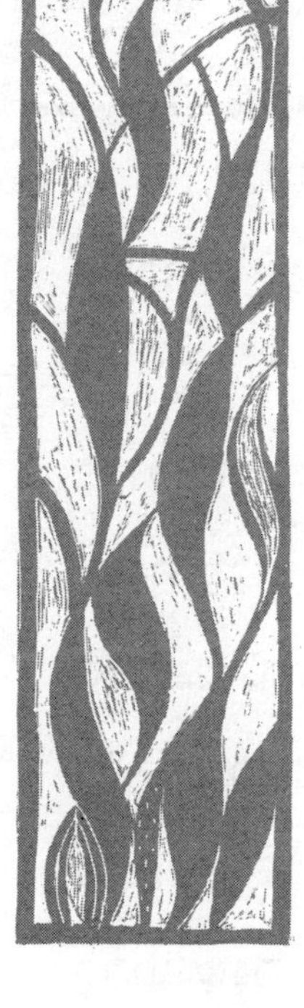

1. They who observe the Sabbath and call it a delight will rejoice in Your kingdom.
2. The people who make the seventh day holy will be satisfied and will delight in Your goodness.
3. You favored the seventh day and declared it holy.
4. You called it the choicest of days, a remembrance of the work of creation.
5. Our God and God of our ancestors, may our Sabbath rest be worthy before You.
6. Sanctify us with Your commandments and may we be among those who are devoted to Your Torah.
7. Satisfy us with Your goodness and cause us to rejoice in Your deliverance.
8. Purify our hearts to serve You in truth.
9. O Lord our God, may we enjoy in love the heritage of Your holy Sabbath,
10. And may the people of Israel who sanctify Your name find rest therein.
11. Praised are You, Lord, who makes the Sabbath holy.

Find and copy the סִדּוּר phrases that contain the words related to שׂ-מ-ח. Write the phrases and their English translations.

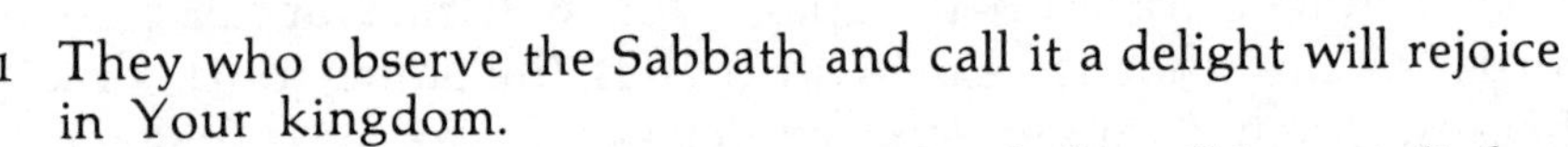

HERE ARE SOME WORDS IN
Lesson Seven

מֶלֶךְ	תּוֹרָה		בָּא
מ־ל־ךְ			ב־ו־א

In each סִדּוּר phrase on this page you will find at least one of these familiar words, or one that is related to it (has the same root). Practice reading these phrases. Then complete the exercises on the next page.

1. כִּי אֵין לָנוּ מֶלֶךְ אֶלָא אַתָּה

2. מַלְכוּתְךָ מַלְכוּת כָּל עוֹלָמִים וּמֶמְשַׁלְתְּךָ בְּכָל דּוֹר וָדוֹר

3. ה׳ מֶלֶךְ, ה׳ מָלָךְ, ה׳ יִמְלֹךְ לְעוֹלָם וָעֶד

4. בָּרוּךְ שֵׁם כְּבוֹד מַלְכוּתוֹ לְעוֹלָם וָעֶד

5. בָּרוּךְ הַבָּא בְּשֵׁם ה׳ בֵּרַכְנוּכֶם מִבֵּית ה׳

6. וַאֲנַחְנוּ כֹּרְעִים וּמִשְׁתַּחֲוִים וּמוֹדִים לִפְנֵי מֶלֶךְ מַלְכֵי הַמְּלָכִים

7. כִּי הַמַּלְכוּת שֶׁלְךָ הִיא, וּלְעוֹלְמֵי עַד תִּמְלֹךְ בְּכָבוֹד

8. כִּי מִצִּיּוֹן תֵּצֵא תוֹרָה וּדְבַר ה׳ מִירוּשָׁלַיִם

9. בָּרוּךְ שֶׁנָּתַן תּוֹרָה לְעַמּוֹ יִשְׂרָאֵל בִּקְדֻשָּׁתוֹ

10. בָּרוּךְ אַתָּה ה׳ נוֹתֵן הַתּוֹרָה

1 In phrase #1 on the opposite page, the word אֶלָּא means *other than, except.* You should understand every other Hebrew word in the phrase.

Write the phrase in your own words:

____

2 The word מַלְכוּת means *kingdom.* It is related to the Hebrew word

_______________ which means _______________.

3 Find ten *different* words that belong to the מ־ל־ך word-family and write

them here. _________ _________ _________ _________

_________ _________ _________ _________

_________ _________ _________ _________

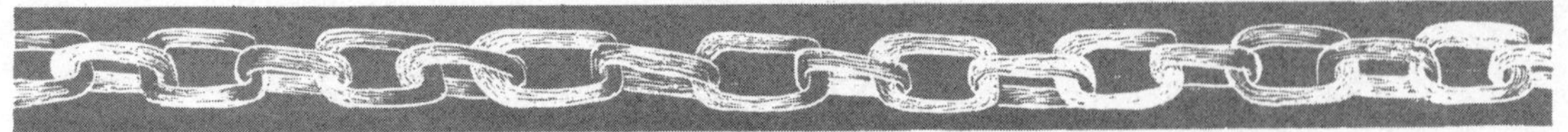

Going out from Egypt

If the Holy One, blessed be He, had not taken our ancestors out of Egypt, then we, and our children, and our children's children would still be enslaved to Pharaoh in Egypt.

That is why we tell the story of יְצִיאַת מִצְרַיִם every year, at פֶּסַח.
We read in the הַגָּדָה:

בְּכָל דּוֹר וָדוֹר חַיָּב אָדָם לִרְאוֹת אֶת עַצְמוֹ כְּאִלּוּ הוּא יָצָא מִמִּצְרָיִם.

In every generation, each person must think of himself or herself as if he or she had gone out of Egypt.

That is why, every time we recite קִדּוּשׁ on שַׁבָּת or on a holiday, we also remind ourselves of יְצִיאַת מִצְרַיִם.

כִּי הוּא יוֹם תְּחִלָּה לְמִקְרָאֵי קֹדֶשׁ, זֵכֶר לִיצִיאַת מִצְרַיִם

יְצִיאַת מִצְרַיִם was one of the most important events in our history as a Jewish people.

לִפְנֵי יְצִיאַת מִצְרַיִם we were עֲבָדִים, slaves.

אַחֲרֵי יְצִיאַת מִצְרַיִם we became a nation — עַם יִשְׂרָאֵל.

Each of us is a link in the very long chain of the Jewish people. Because of the way our families chose to live in past generations, we ourselves are members of a large family called the Jewish people. In every generation people do things that affect all the generations that follow them.

Here is part of a תְּפִלָּה that we find in the הַגָּדָה. We read it at the Passover seder, סֵדֶר שֶׁל פֶּסַח.

He took us	הוֹצִיאָנוּ
from slavery to freedom	מֵעַבְדוּת לְחֵרוּת
from despair to joy	מִיָּגוֹן לְשִׂמְחָה
from mourning to celebration	מֵאֵבֶל לְיוֹם טוֹב
and from darkness to great light	וּמֵאֲפֵלָה לְאוֹר גָּדוֹל
and from enslavement to redemption	וּמִשְׁעְבּוּד לִגְאֻלָה
and we shall chant before Him	וְנֹאמַר לְפָנָיו
a new song. Halleluyah.	שִׁירָה חֲדָשָׁה. הַלְלוּיָהּ.

Underline all the Hebrew prefixes that mean *from*.
Circle all the Hebrew prefixes that mean *to*.

CHALLENGE QUESTIONS

1 Who is the *He* in this תְּפִלָּה? ——————————— Who is the *us*?

————————————————————————————

2 What do you think *"we shall chant before Him a new song"* means?

————————————————————————————

(Hint: הַלְלוּיָהּ means *Praise God!*)

3 Why do you think this תְּפִלָּה says that *we* were redeemed from slavery in Egypt? ———————————

————————————————————————————

עָלֵינוּ

When we recite the עָלֵינוּ prayer, we praise and thank God — אֲדוֹן הַכֹּל — the Lord of all things. We bend our knees to show our respect for מֶלֶךְ מַלְכֵי הַמְּלָכִים — the supreme King of kings.

1 עָלֵינוּ לְשַׁבֵּחַ לַאֲדוֹן הַכֹּל לָתֵת גְּדֻלָּה לְיוֹצֵר בְּרֵאשִׁית,

2 שֶׁלֹּא עָשָׂנוּ כְּגוֹיֵי הָאֲרָצוֹת וְלֹא שָׂמָנוּ כְּמִשְׁפְּחוֹת הָאֲדָמָה.

3 שֶׁלֹּא שָׂם חֶלְקֵנוּ כָּהֶם וְגוֹרָלֵנוּ כְּכָל הֲמוֹנָם.

4 וַאֲנַחְנוּ כּוֹרְעִים וּמִשְׁתַּחֲוִים וּמוֹדִים

5 לִפְנֵי מֶלֶךְ מַלְכֵי הַמְּלָכִים הַקָּדוֹשׁ בָּרוּךְ הוּא.

6 שֶׁהוּא נוֹטֶה שָׁמַיִם וְיוֹסֵד אָרֶץ

7 וּמוֹשַׁב יְקָרוֹ בַּשָּׁמַיִם מִמַּעַל וּשְׁכִינַת עֻזּוֹ בְּגָבְהֵי מְרוֹמִים.

8 הוּא אֱלֹהֵינוּ אֵין עוֹד.

9 אֱמֶת מַלְכֵּנוּ אֶפֶס זוּלָתוֹ.

10 כַּכָּתוּב בְּתוֹרָתוֹ. וְיָדַעְתָּ הַיּוֹם וַהֲשֵׁבֹתָ אֶל לְבָבֶךָ

11 כִּי יְיָ הוּא הָאֱלֹהִים בַּשָּׁמַיִם מִמַּעַל וְעַל הָאָרֶץ מִתָּחַת

12 אֵין עוֹד.

1 It is for us to praise the Lord of all things, to acclaim the Creator of all existence.

2 He did not make like us the heathen of the earth, He did not fashion us like the pagans of the world.

3 Our portion is not like theirs, our lot is not like that of their multitudes.

4 We bend the knee, bow down, and give thanks

5 To the supreme King of kings, the Holy One, praised be He.

6 It is He who stretched forth the heavens and laid the foundations of the earth.

7 His glorious Presence is in the heavens above; the dominion of His might is in the loftiest heights.

8 He is our God; there is none else.

9 He is our true King; there is none other.

10 As it is written in His Torah: And you shall know this day and meditate in your heart,

11 That the Lord is God in the heavens above and on the earth beneath.

12 There is none else.

1 Copy the Hebrew line that calls God the Ruler (Lord) of all the world.

2 Copy the Hebrew line which shows our deep respect for God, the King of kings.

HERE ARE SOME WORDS IN
Lesson Eight

אָמַר	צַוָּה	מִצְוָה	דִּבְרֵי	קֹדֶשׁ	לַעֲשׂוֹת
א־מ־ר	צ־ו־ה		ד־ב־ר	ק־ד־שׁ	ע־שׂ־ה

In each סִדּוּר phrase on this page you will find at least one of these familiar words, or one that is related to it (has the same root). Practice reading these phrases. Then complete the exercises on the next page.

1 בָּרוּךְ שֶׁאָמַר וְהָיָה הָעוֹלָם, בָּרוּךְ הוּא

2 בָּרוּךְ אוֹמֵר וְעוֹשֶׂה

3 וְשָׁמְרוּ בְנֵי יִשְׂרָאֵל אֶת הַשַּׁבָּת, לַעֲשׂוֹת אֶת הַשַּׁבָּת לְדֹרוֹתָם

4 הֲדַר כְּבוֹד הוֹדֶךָ וְדִבְרֵי נִפְלְאֹתֶיךָ אָשִׂיחָה

5 וְהָיוּ הַדְּבָרִים הָאֵלֶּה אֲשֶׁר אָנֹכִי מְצַוְּךָ הַיּוֹם עַל לְבָבֶךָ

6 תּוֹרָה צִוָּה לָנוּ מֹשֶׁה, מוֹרָשָׁה קְהִלַּת יַעֲקֹב

7 וַיְבָרֶךְ אֱלֹהִים אֶת יוֹם הַשְּׁבִיעִי וַיְקַדֵּשׁ אוֹתוֹ

8 בָּרוּךְ אַתָּה ה׳ אֱלֹהֵינוּ מֶלֶךְ הָעוֹלָם

9 שֶׁעָשָׂה נִסִּים לַאֲבוֹתֵינוּ בַּיָּמִים הָהֵם בַּזְּמַן הַזֶּה

10 עֹשֶׂה שָׁלוֹם בִּמְרוֹמָיו, הוּא יַעֲשֶׂה שָׁלוֹם עָלֵינוּ וְעַל כָּל יִשְׂרָאֵל

1 The בְּרָכָה on lines #8 and #9 is said on חֲנֻכָּה and on פּוּרִים. It praises and thanks God *who did miracles for our ancestors in those days at this time.* Write the Hebrew words that mean *who did miracles for our ancestors.* (Look for a word in the ע־ש־ה family!)

_______________   _______________   _________

2 Which familiar words do you recognize in בַּיָּמִים הָהֵם בַּזְּמַן הַזֶּה?

__________   __________   __________   __________

3 What does line #2 mean?___________________________________

A בְּרָכָה for a מִצְוָה

Some בְּרָכוֹת are said when we do something that God has commanded us to do. These are בְּרָכוֹת שֶׁל מִצְוָה, and each one begins with the same ten words.

בָּרוּךְ אַתָּה ה׳ אֱלֹהֵינוּ מֶלֶךְ הָעוֹלָם אֲשֶׁר קִדְּשָׁנוּ בְּמִצְוֹתָיו וְצִוָּנוּ

You are blessed, Lord, our God, King of the world,
who has sanctified us with His commandments and commanded us...

Here is a בְּרָכָה שֶׁל מִצְוָה that is said when we prepare to study תּוֹרָה.

בָּרוּךְ אַתָּה ה׳ אֱלֹהֵינוּ מֶלֶךְ הָעוֹלָם
אֲשֶׁר קִדְּשָׁנוּ בְּמִצְוֹתָיו וְצִוָּנוּ לַעֲסֹק בְּדִבְרֵי תּוֹרָה

You are blessed, Lord, our God, King of the world,
who has sanctified us with His commandments and commanded us
to engage in words of Torah.

Why do you think engaging in the words of Torah is a מִצְוָה?

____

Write any בְּרָכָה you know that is said before eating something.

____

____

What do these words mean?

____

____

בִּרְכוֹת שֶׁל מִצְוָה

Here are four בְּרָכוֹת that are said on special occasions.

1 בָּרוּךְ אַתָּה ה׳ אֱלֹהֵינוּ מֶלֶךְ הָעוֹלָם
אֲשֶׁר קִדְּשָׁנוּ בְּמִצְוֹתָיו וְצִוָּנוּ עַל אֲכִילַת מַצָּה.

2 בָּרוּךְ אַתָּה ה׳ אֱלֹהֵינוּ מֶלֶךְ הָעוֹלָם
אֲשֶׁר קִדְּשָׁנוּ בְּמִצְוֹתָיו וְצִוָּנוּ לִשְׁמֹעַ קוֹל שׁוֹפָר.

3 בָּרוּךְ אַתָּה ה׳ אֱלֹהֵינוּ מֶלֶךְ הָעוֹלָם
אֲשֶׁר קִדְּשָׁנוּ בְּמִצְוֹתָיו וְצִוָּנוּ עַל מִקְרָא מְגִלָּה.

4 בָּרוּךְ אַתָּה ה׳ אֱלֹהֵינוּ מֶלֶךְ הָעוֹלָם
אֲשֶׁר קִדְּשָׁנוּ בְּמִצְוֹתָיו וְצִוָּנוּ לֵישֵׁב בַּסֻּכָּה.

1 When do we recite each of these בְּרָכוֹת? (You don't have to understand *every* word in order to know the answer. There is a clue word in each בְּרָכָה.)

1. _______________________ 2. _______________________

3. _______________________ 4. _______________________

2 How do we know that each of these בְּרָכוֹת is a בְּרָכָה שֶׁל מִצְוָה?

____

3 Are these personal בְּרָכוֹת (*I* am saying it), or community (group) בְּרָכוֹת (*we* are saying it)? _______________________

How do you know this? _______________________

פְּסוּקֵי דְזִמְרָא

At the beginning of the morning service, we praise God for the many wonderful things He does. The תְּפִלָה is called פְּסוּקֵי דְזִמְרָא — Verses of Song.

1 בָּרוּךְ שֶׁאָמַר וְהָיָה הָעוֹלָם בָּרוּךְ הוּא.

2 בָּרוּךְ עוֹשֶׂה בְרֵאשִׁית.

3 בָּרוּךְ אוֹמֵר וְעוֹשֶׂה.

4 בָּרוּךְ גוֹזֵר וּמְקַיֵם.

5 בָּרוּךְ מְרַחֵם עַל הָאָרֶץ.

6 בָּרוּךְ מְרַחֵם עַל הַבְּרִיוֹת.

7 בָּרוּךְ מְשַׁלֵם שָׂכָר טוֹב לִירֵאָיו:

8 בָּרוּךְ חַי לָעַד וְקַיָם לָנֶצַח.

9 בָּרוּךְ פּוֹדֶה וּמַצִיל בָּרוּךְ שְׁמוֹ.

1 Praised be He, whose word created the universe, praised be He.

2 Praised be He, who created all things in the beginning.

3 Praised be He, who fulfills His promises.

4 Praised be He, who carries out His decrees.

5 Praised be He, who is merciful toward the earth.

6 Praised be He, who is merciful toward His creatures.

7 Praised be He, who rewards those that revere Him.

8 Praised be He, who lives forever and exists to all eternity.

9 Praised be He, who redeems and rescues, praised be His name.

1 We are created in God's image. We can try to imitate God's ways. Study the English translation of פְּסוּקֵי דְזִמְרָא and list the things mentioned that you can try to imitate.

_________________________   _________________________

_________________________   _________________________

2 Of all of the things mentioned in this תְּפִלָה, which do you think is most important? Find the Hebrew line that expresses the idea you have selected and copy the Hebrew line.

____

HERE ARE SOME WORDS IN
Lesson Nine

| שַׁבָּת | מְלָאכָה | יום | בָּרָא | שָׁמַיִם |
| שׁ־ב־ת | | | ב־ר־א | |

In each סִדוּר phrase on this page you will find at least one of these familiar words, or one that is related to it (has the same root). Practice reading these phrases. Then complete the exercises on the next page.

1 אֲדוֹן עוֹלָם אֲשֶׁר מָלַךְ בְּטֶרֶם כָּל יְצִיר נִבְרָא

2 טוֹבִים מְאוֹרוֹת שֶׁבָּרָא אֱלֹהֵינוּ

3 כִּי שֵׁשֶׁת יָמִים עָשָׂה ה׳ אֶת הַשָּׁמַיִם וְאֶת הָאָרֶץ

4 וּבַיּוֹם הַשְּׁבִיעִי שָׁבַת וַיִּנָּפַשׁ

5 שֵׁשֶׁת יָמִים תַּעֲבֹד וְעָשִׂיתָ כָּל מְלַאכְתֶּךָ

6 וְיוֹם הַשְּׁבִיעִי שַׁבָּת לַה׳ אֱלֹהֶיךָ, לֹא תַעֲשֶׂה כָּל מְלָאכָה

7 הַשָּׁמַיִם מְסַפְּרִים כְּבוֹד אֵל

8 וַיְכֻלּוּ הַשָּׁמַיִם וְהָאָרֶץ וְכָל צְבָאָם

9 עַל כֵּן בֵּרַךְ ה׳ אֶת יוֹם הַשַּׁבָּת וַיְקַדְּשֵׁהוּ

10 כִּי הוּא הָאֱלֹהִים בַּשָּׁמַיִם מִמַּעַל וְעַל הָאָרֶץ מִתַּחַת, אֵין עוֹד

1 In phrase #10 on the opposite page, מִמַּעַל means *above*, and מִתַּחַת means *below*. Write the meaning of this תְּפִלָה._______________

____

2 We have learned that God is described as
טוֹב, גָדוֹל, מֶלֶךְ, בּוֹרֵא אֶת הַכֹּל
Which of these qualities of God does phrase #10 describe? _______________

3 Find two phrases that tell us that God is the Creator. #— #—
Which words in the ב-ר-א family provided the clue?

_______________   _______________

Praying together

Why do we have to go to בֵּית הַכְּנֶסֶת to pray? Can't we pray to God by ourselves? Of course we can. People can think or say or sing a prayer to God wherever they may be. God hears all prayers. ה׳ שׁוֹמֵעַ תְּפִלָּה.

But when we pray together, as a large Jewish family, we know that we are not alone. Our family, our friends, our neighbors, are alongside us, reciting the same words, thinking many of the same thoughts and sharing the same hopes.

We read in the סדור that all Jews are friends. חֲבֵרִים כָּל יִשְׂרָאֵל

When we open the סדור, we know that throughout the world, wherever there is a Jewish community — small or large — our fellow Jews are saying and singing the same תְּפִלוֹת. In fact, most of the תְּפִלוֹת in the סדור are written in the plural form. In them

We thank God for His goodness to *us*.

We ask that He bless *us* with health and peace.

We ask God to forgive *us* if we have not followed His commandments, and if we have forgotten that we are created in God's image.

כִּי בְּצֶלֶם אֱלֹהִים נִבְרָא הָאָדָם.

Some תְּפִלּוֹת in the סִדּוּר are personal prayers, written in the singular form. You can recognize these prayers by the words ending in ־ִי. or ־ִ. (You know the word שֶׁלִי which means *my*.)

Here are two examples.

1 אֱלֹהַי, נְצוֹר לְשׁוֹנִי מֵרָע, וּשְׂפָתַי מִדַּבֵּר מִרְמָה.

2 פְּתַח לִבִּי בְּתוֹרָתֶךָ, וּבְמִצְוֹתֶיךָ תִּרְדֹּף נַפְשִׁי.

1 My God, guard my tongue from evil, and my lips from speaking falsehood.

2 Open my heart to Your Torah, and may my soul seek to follow Your commandments.

CHALLENGE QUESTIONS

1 Use your own words to write the idea in תְּפִלָה #1.

God, please help me ______________

____

2 What would happen if we did not act this way? ______________

____

3 Do you think תְּפִלָה #2 *is a good* תְּפִלָה? Why?

____

4 Make up a personal prayer of your own, in English.

Write it here. ______________

____

We talk to God

The שִׂים שָׁלוֹם prayer is one in which we talk to God.

1 שִׂים שָׁלוֹם טוֹבָה וּבְרָכָה

2 חֵן נָחֶסֶד וְרַחֲמִים עָלֵינוּ וְעַל כָּל יִשְׂרָאֵל עַמֶּךָ.

3 בָּרְכֵנוּ אָבִינוּ כֻּלָנוּ כְּאֶחָד בְּאוֹר פָּנֶיךָ

4 כִּי בְאוֹר פָּנֶיךָ נָתַתָּ לָנוּ ה׳ אֱלֹהֵינוּ תּוֹרַת חַיִּים

5 וְאַהֲבַת חֶסֶד, וּצְדָקָה וּבְרָכָה וְרַחֲמִים וְחַיִּים וְשָׁלוֹם.

1 Grant us peace, happiness and blessing,

2 grace and loving-kindness and mercy; grant them to us and to Your people Israel.

3 Our Father, bless us one and all with the light of Your presence;

4 for by that light, Lord our God, You have given us the Torah of life,

5 love of mercy, justice, blessing, compassion, life and peace.

1 Underline all the words that show *we* are talking (remember — the suffix נוּ means *we, us*).

2 Use your own words to make a list of all the things we ask God to give us in the שִׂים שָׁלוֹם prayer.

____

____

3 Are there any things you would like to add to this list?

____

God talks to us

Here is part of a תְּפִלָה that is said every single day, after singing
שְׁמַע יִשְׂרָאֵל ה׳ אֱלֹהֵינוּ ה׳ אֶחָד.
This is a תְּפִלָה in which God is speaking to us.

1 וְהָיָה אִם שָׁמֹעַ תִּשְׁמְעוּ אֶל מִצְוֹתַי

2 אֲשֶׁר אָנֹכִי מְצַוֶּה אֶתְכֶם הַיוֹם

3 לְאַהֲבָה אֶת ה׳ אֱלֹהֵיכֶם וּלְעָבְדוֹ

4 בְּכָל לְבַבְכֶם וּבְכָל נַפְשְׁכֶם —

5 וְנָתַתִּי מְטַר אַרְצְכֶם בְּעִתּוֹ.

1 If you will listen and obey My commandments

2 which I command you this day

3 to love the Lord your God and serve Him

4 with all your heart and soul —

5 I will give rain for your land at the proper season.

This תְּפִלָה comes from the Bible. You can find it in the Book of Deuteronomy, chapter 11, verses 13-14. It is so important that it is written on the parchment found inside the מְזוּזָה we place on our doorposts. When we see the מְזוּזָה we are reminded that God tells us to *obey* His commandments, and to *love* Him.

אַתָּה הוּא

This תְּפִלָּה is recited every morning. Practice reading the תְּפִלָּה.

1 אַתָּה הוּא, יְיָ אֱלֹהֵינוּ, בַּשָּׁמַיִם וּבָאָרֶץ וּבִשְׁמֵי הַשָּׁמַיִם הָעֶלְיוֹנִים.

2 אֱמֶת, אַתָּה הוּא רִאשׁוֹן וְאַתָּה הוּא אַחֲרוֹן,

3 וּמִבַּלְעָדֶיךָ אֵין אֱלֹהִים.

4 קַבֵּץ קוֶיךָ מֵאַרְבַּע כַּנְפוֹת הָאָרֶץ.

5 יַכִּירוּ וְיֵדְעוּ כָּל בָּאֵי עוֹלָם כִּי אַתָּה הוּא הָאֱלֹהִים לְבַדְּךָ לְכֹל מַמְלְכוֹת הָאָרֶץ.

6 אַתָּה עָשִׂיתָ אֶת הַשָּׁמַיִם וְאֶת הָאָרֶץ, אֶת הַיָּם, וְאֶת כָּל אֲשֶׁר בָּם,

7 וּמִי בְּכָל מַעֲשֵׂה יָדֶיךָ, בָּעֶלְיוֹנִים אוֹ בַתַּחְתּוֹנִים, שֶׁיֹּאמַר לְךָ מַה תַּעֲשֶׂה.

1 O Lord our God, You alone are sovereign in the farthest spaces of the heavens, as on the earth below.

2 You were before creation began, and You will be unto all eternity.

3 Besides You there is no God.

4 Restore the homeless of our people, who have placed their trust in You, from the four corners of the earth.

5 Let all people know that You alone are Sovereign over all the nations of the world.

6 You have fashioned the heavens and the earth, the sea, and all that is within them.

7 Who among Your creatures, in heaven or on earth, can tell You how to act?

1 Copy the Hebrew line that tells us that God made everything in the world. 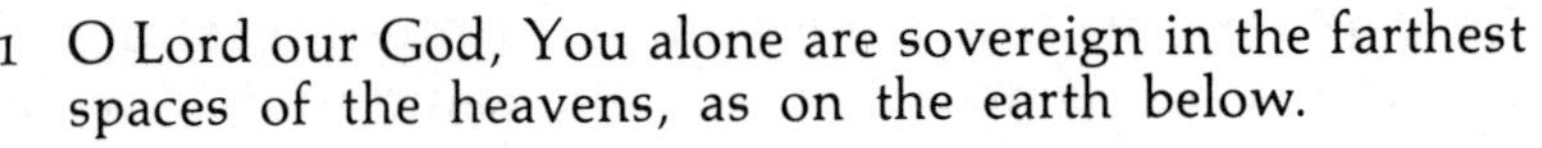

2 After we praise God's greatness in this תְּפִלָה, we ask God for something. Find the English translation of our request and write it here. —————————————

3 Why do you think Jews have recited this prayer every morning, for generations and generations? —————————————

Lesson Ten

בְּרָצוֹן עֶרֶב יִשְׂרָאֵל אַהֲבָה כֻּלָּנוּ כּוֹס

א־ה־ב

In each סִדּוּר phrase on this page you will find at least one of these familiar words, or one that is related to it (has the same root). Practice reading these phrases. Then complete the exercises on the next page.

1 וּתְפִלָּתָם בְּאַהֲבָה תְקַבֵּל בְּרָצוֹן

2 וּתְהִי לְרָצוֹן תָּמִיד עֲבוֹדַת יִשְׂרָאֵל עַמֶּךָ

3 יְהִי רָצוֹן מִלְּפָנֶיךָ ה'...שֶׁתַּעֲלֵנוּ בְּשִׂמְחָה לְאַרְצֵנוּ

4 כּוֹס יְשׁוּעוֹת אֶשָּׂא וּבְשֵׁם ה' אֶקְרָא

5 אַהֲבָה רַבָּה אוֹתָנוּ אֲהַבְתָּנוּ

6 עֶרֶב וָבֹקֶר בְּכָל יוֹם תָּמִיד פַּעֲמַיִם בְּאַהֲבָה "שְׁמַע" אוֹמְרִים

7 בָּרְכֵנוּ אָבִינוּ כֻּלָּנוּ כְּאֶחָד בְּאוֹר פָּנֶיךָ

8 הוּא יַעֲשֶׂה שָׁלוֹם עָלֵינוּ וְעַל כָּל יִשְׂרָאֵל, וְאִמְרוּ "אָמֵן"

9 בָּרוּךְ אַתָּה ה' הַמְבָרֵךְ אֶת עַמּוֹ יִשְׂרָאֵל בַּשָּׁלוֹם.

10 שֶׁבְּכָל הַלֵּילוֹת אָנוּ אוֹכְלִין בֵּין יוֹשְׁבִין וּבֵין מְסֻבִּין

הַלַּיְלָה הַזֶּה כֻּלָּנוּ מְסֻבִּין.

1 Phrase #3 asks God to bring us בְּשִׂמְחָה לְאַרְצֵנוּ.

What familiar word do you see in אַרְצֵנוּ? ________________

What does it mean? ____________ What does the נוּ ending mean?

____

Now you know that אַרְצֵנוּ means ________.

What is the geographical name of אַרְצֵנוּ? ________________

Why do we call it אַרְצֵנוּ? ________________

2 In phrase #7 you will find the word כֻּלָנוּ.
Divide this word into a familiar word, and a suffix (word ending).

The ending is ________. The word is ________.

Now you know that כֻּלָנוּ means ________.

God's holiness

When we recite קִדּוּשׁ at home, we sanctify (make holy) the שַׁבָּת or a holiday. To *sanctify* or *make holy* means to *set apart*, to *make special*.

שַׁבָּת and holidays are special days, set apart from the other days of the week or year.

There is something that is so special, so sanctified, so קָדוֹשׁ, that it alone is set apart from everything else in the world. That is the one God. Nothing else is like Him.

ה׳ אֶחָד, אֵין כָּמוֹךָ בָּאֵלִים ה׳

Another name for God is *the Holy One, blessed be He.*

הַקָּדוֹשׁ בָּרוּךְ הוּא

Whenever we remind ourselves of God's holiness, of the very special nature of God, we praise Him. That is why, when we are in בֵּית הַכְּנֶסֶת and God's name is praised in these words

...,בָּרוּךְ אַתָּה ה׳

we very often respond, all together,

בָּרוּךְ הוּא וּבָרוּךְ שְׁמוֹ

which means *praised is He, praised is His Name.*

הַקָּדוֹשׁ בָּרוּךְ הוּא

Here is a תְּפִלָּה about הַקָּדוֹשׁ בָּרוּךְ הוּא.

1 אַתָּה קָדוֹשׁ וְשִׁמְךָ קָדוֹשׁ

2 וּקְדוֹשִׁים בְּכָל יוֹם יְהַלְלוּךָ, סֶלָה.*

3 בָּרוּךְ אַתָּה ה', הָאֵל הַקָּדוֹשׁ.

You know almost all the words in this תְּפִלָּה. Fill in the blanks and read the תְּפִלָּה in English.

1. _______________________________

2. and the holy ones will praise You every day, Sela.*

3. _______________________________

We are not sure of the meaning of סֶלָה. We think it is a musical signal. In ancient Jerusalem, the Levites stood on the steps leading up to the Temple and sang Psalms in praise of God. Whenever we say the word סֶלָה in our תְּפִלּוֹת, we are reminded of how our ancestors prayed at the Temple in Jerusalem.

In the תְּפִלָּה the *holy ones* are the Jewish people. In the תְּפִלָּה we read that God told Moses: ''Speak to all the congregation of the Children of Israel and say to them, 'You shall be holy; for I, the Lord your God, am holy.' ''

CHALLENGE QUESTIONS

1 What is the name given to the Children of Israel today

____

2 Give an example of how we can be ''holy'' today. _______________

____

Holy, holy, holy is God

The תְּפִלָּה in which we proclaim that God is sanctified is called קְדֻשָׁה. This תְּפִלָּה is so special that we are permitted to recite קְדֻשָׁה only with a מִנְיָן of ten Jews.

Here is the קְדֻשָׁה that is part of the *Amidah* prayer said every morning.

נְקַדֵּשׁ אֶת שִׁמְךָ בָּעוֹלָם, כְּשֵׁם שֶׁמַּקְדִּישִׁים אוֹתוֹ בִּשְׁמֵי מָרוֹם,

כַּכָּתוּב עַל יַד נְבִיאֶךָ, וְקָרָא זֶה אֶל זֶה וְאָמַר:

קָדוֹשׁ, קָדוֹשׁ, קָדוֹשׁ, ה' צְבָאוֹת

מְלֹא כָל הָאָרֶץ כְּבוֹדוֹ.

לְעֻמָּתָם בָּרוּךְ יֹאמֵרוּ:

בָּרוּךְ כְּבוֹד ה' מִמְּקוֹמוֹ.

וּבְדִבְרֵי קָדְשְׁךָ כָּתוּב לֵאמֹר:

יִמְלֹךְ ה' לְעוֹלָם, אֱלֹהַיִךְ צִיּוֹן, לְדֹר וָדֹר, הַלְלוּיָהּ.

לְדוֹר וָדוֹר נַגִּיד גָּדְלֶךָ, וּלְנֵצַח נְצָחִים קְדֻשָּׁתְךָ נַקְדִּישׁ.

וְשִׁבְחֲךָ אֱלֹהֵינוּ מִפִּינוּ לֹא יָמוּשׁ לְעוֹלָם וָעֶד,

כִּי אֵל מֶלֶךְ גָּדוֹל וְקָדוֹשׁ אָתָּה.

בָּרוּךְ אַתָּה ה', הָאֵל הַקָּדוֹשׁ.

The right בְּרָכָה at the right time

When do we say these בְּרָכוֹת?

1 בָּרוּךְ אַתָּה ה׳ אֱלֹהֵינוּ מֶלֶךְ הָעוֹלָם
בּוֹרֵא פְּרִי הַגָּפֶן.

2 בָּרוּךְ אַתָּה ה׳ אֱלֹהֵינוּ מֶלֶךְ הָעוֹלָם
בּוֹרֵא פְּרִי הָאֲדָמָה.

3 בָּרוּךְ אַתָּה ה׳ אֱלֹהֵינוּ מֶלֶךְ הָעוֹלָם
בּוֹרֵא מִינֵי מְזוֹנוֹת.

4 בָּרוּךְ אַתָּה ה׳ אֱלֹהֵינוּ מֶלֶךְ הָעוֹלָם
בּוֹרֵא פְּרִי הָעֵץ.

5 בָּרוּךְ אַתָּה ה׳ אֱלֹהֵינוּ מֶלֶךְ הָעוֹלָם
בּוֹרֵא מִינֵי בְשָׂמִים.

6 בָּרוּךְ אַתָּה ה׳ אֱלֹהֵינוּ מֶלֶךְ הָעוֹלָם
אֲשֶׁר קִדְּשָׁנוּ בְּמִצְוֹתָיו וְצִוָּנוּ
לְהַדְלִיק נֵר שֶׁל שַׁבָּת.

7 בָּרוּךְ אַתָּה ה׳ אֱלֹהֵינוּ מֶלֶךְ הָעוֹלָם
אֲשֶׁר קִדְּשָׁנוּ בְּמִצְוֹתָיו וְצִוָּנוּ
עַל אֲכִילַת מַצָּה.

8 בָּרוּךְ אַתָּה ה׳ אֱלֹהֵינוּ מֶלֶךְ הָעוֹלָם
אֲשֶׁר קִדְּשָׁנוּ בְּמִצְוֹתָיו וְצִוָּנוּ
לֵישֵׁב בַּסֻּכָּה.

אַהֲבַת עוֹלָם

In the evening service, we read a beautiful תְּפִלָה called אַהֲבַת עוֹלָם.
Practice reading this תְּפִלָה.

1 אַהֲבַת עוֹלָם בֵּית יִשְׂרָאֵל עַמְךָ אָהָבְתָּ.

2 תּוֹרָה וּמִצְוֹת חֻקִּים וּמִשְׁפָּטִים אוֹתָנוּ לִמַּדְתָּ.

3 עַל־כֵּן יְיָ אֱלֹהֵינוּ בְּשָׁכְבֵּנוּ וּבְקוּמֵנוּ נָשִׂיחַ בְּחֻקֶּיךָ.

4 וְנִשְׂמַח בְּדִבְרֵי תוֹרָתְךָ וּבְמִצְוֹתֶיךָ לְעוֹלָם וָעֶד.

5 כִּי הֵם חַיֵּינוּ וְאֹרֶךְ יָמֵינוּ

6 וּבָהֶם נֶהְגֶה יוֹמָם וָלָיְלָה.

7 וְאַהֲבָתְךָ אַל תָּסִיר מִמֶּנוּ לְעוֹלָמִים.

8 בָּרוּךְ אַתָּה יְיָ אוֹהֵב עַמּוֹ יִשְׂרָאֵל:

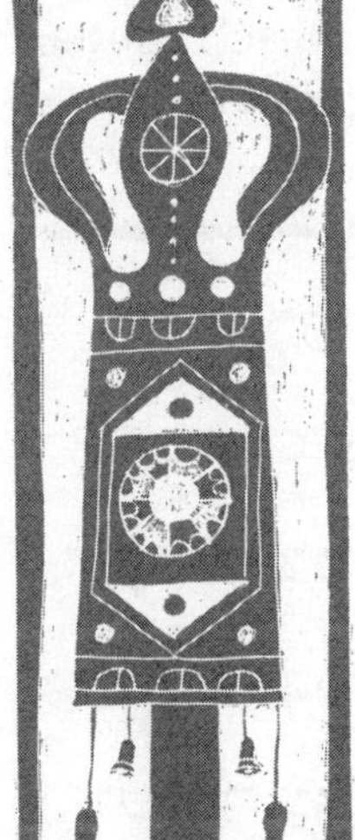

1 With everlasting love You have loved the house of Israel.

2 You have revealed to us the Law and commandments, statutes and judgments.

3 Therefore, Lord our God, when we lie down and when we rise up we shall speak of Your statutes.

4 We shall rejoice in the words of Your Law and in Your commandments forever and ever.

5 For they are our life and the measure of our days

6 And we will meditate on them day and night.

7 May You never take away Your love from us.

8 Praised are You, Lord, who loves Your people Israel.

1 Copy the Hebrew lines that say:
God loves the House of Israel

God expresses this love through the gifts of תּוֹרָה and מִצְוֹת.

2 Can you explain how the תּוֹרָה and מִצְוֹת are an expression

of God's love for us?

HERE ARE SOME WORDS IN
Lesson Eleven

לְהַדְלִיק	נֵר, נֵרוֹת	שׁוֹמֵר	בָּחַרְתָּ	עַמִּים	עַם,
		שׁ־מ־ר	ב־ח־ר		

In each סִדוּר phrase on this page you will find at least one of these familiar words, or one that is related to it (has the same root). Practice reading these phrases. Then complete the exercises on the next page.

1 כִּי בָנוּ בָחַרְתָּ וְאוֹתָנוּ קִדַּשְׁתָּ מִכָּל הָעַמִּים

2 שׁוֹמֵר ה' אֶת כָּל אֹהֲבָיו וְאֵת כָּל הָרְשָׁעִים יַשְׁמִיד

3 וְשָׁמְרוּ בְּנֵי יִשְׂרָאֵל אֶת הַשַּׁבָּת

4 יִשְׂמְחוּ בְמַלְכוּתְךָ שׁוֹמְרֵי שַׁבָּת וְקוֹרְאֵי עֹנֶג

5 וּשְׁמוֹר צֵאתֵנוּ וּבוֹאֵנוּ לְחַיִּים וּלְשָׁלוֹם, מֵעַתָּה וְעַד עוֹלָם

6 כִּי אַתָּה שׁוֹמֵעַ תְּפִלּוֹת עַמְּךָ יִשְׂרָאֵל

7 רְצֵה ה' אֱלֹהֵינוּ בְּעַמְּךָ יִשְׂרָאֵל וּבִתְפִלָּתָם

8 וּתְהִי לְרָצוֹן תָּמִיד עֲבוֹדַת יִשְׂרָאֵל עַמֶּךָ

9 בָּרוּךְ אַתָּה ה' אֱלֹהֵינוּ מֶלֶךְ הָעוֹלָם, אֲשֶׁר בָּחַר בָּנוּ מִכָּל הָעַמִּים

וְנָתַן לָנוּ אֶת תּוֹרָתוֹ.

10 בָּרוּךְ אַתָּה ה' אֱלֹהֵינוּ מֶלֶךְ הָעוֹלָם, אֲשֶׁר קִדְּשָׁנוּ בְּמִצְוֹתָיו וְצִוָּנוּ

לְהַדְלִיק נֵר שֶׁל שַׁבָּת.

1 Find four phrases on the opposite page that include a word from the ש־מ־ר family. Write the words here. _____________ _____________

_____________ _____________

2 If עַם means _____________, then עַמְּךָ means _____________.

Who is the *Your* in the סִדוּר? _____________

Who is the עַם or עַמְּךָ? _____________

3 When do we say the בְּרָכָה on line #10? _____________
On what other occasions do we recite a בְּרָכָה over נֵרוֹת?

Give as many examples as you can: _____________

____

What can God do?

1 ה׳ אוֹמֵר וְעוֹשֶׂה

2 ה׳ עָשָׂה שָׁמַיִם וָאָרֶץ

3 ה׳ עָשָׂה עֶרֶב וָבֹקֶר

4 ה׳ עָשָׂה עֵצִים וּפְרָחִים

5 ה׳ עָשָׂה אֶת כָּל הַחַיּוֹת

6 ה׳ עָשָׂה אִישׁ וְאִשָּׁה, אָדָם וְחַוָּה

7 ה׳ עָשָׂה אֶת הַכֹּל בָּעוֹלָם

Think about it....

1 What are some of the things you can do?

____

____

2 What can't you do?

____

____

3 What is the important difference between man and God?

____

____

God protects us

From the סִדּוּר we know that God is טוֹב and גָּדוֹל. We know that because He is מֶלֶךְ מַלְכֵי הַמְּלָכִים, He is powerful.

The תְּפִלּוֹת in the סִדּוּר also tell us that God protects or guards us.

Read these סִדּוּר phrases and circle all the words that tell us that God is a protector.

1 שׁוֹמֵר ה׳ אֶת כָּל אֹהֲבָיו

2 וּשְׁמוֹר צֵאתֵנוּ וּבוֹאֵנוּ לְחַיִּים וּלְשָׁלוֹם

3 שׁוֹמֵר יִשְׂרָאֵל, שְׁמוֹר שְׁאֵרִית יִשְׂרָאֵל

You know many of these Hebrew words. Read each סִדּוּר phrase again, and fill in the blanks to complete the phrases in English. (Remember, look for a familiar or related word.)

1. God _________ those who _________ Him

2. _________ our going out and our coming in for _______ and for

____

3. _______________, of _______ the remnant of _________

CHALLENGE QUESTIONS

1 What do you think *our going out and our coming in* means?

____

What do we ask God to do throughout the day?

____

2 A *remnant* is a small amount that is left from a much larger amount (a remainder). Why do we talk about *the remnant of Israel*?

____

3 How do you feel when you know that God protects us?

____

קִדּוּשׁ שֶׁל שַׁבָּת

1 בָּרוּךְ אַתָּה ה׳ אֱלֹהֵינוּ מֶלֶךְ הָעוֹלָם,

2 אֲשֶׁר קִדְּשָׁנוּ בְּמִצְוֹתָיו וְרָצָה בָנוּ,

3 וְשַׁבַּת קָדְשׁוֹ בְּאַהֲבָה וּבְרָצוֹן הִנְחִילָנוּ,

4 זִכָּרוֹן לְמַעֲשֵׂה בְרֵאשִׁית.

5 כִּי הוּא יוֹם תְּחִלָּה לְמִקְרָאֵי קֹדֶשׁ

6 זֵכֶר לִיצִיאַת מִצְרָיִם.

7 כִּי בָנוּ בָחַרְתָּ וְאוֹתָנוּ קִדַּשְׁתָּ מִכָּל הָעַמִּים

8 וְשַׁבַּת קָדְשְׁךָ בְּאַהֲבָה וּבְרָצוֹן הִנְחַלְתָּנוּ.

9 בָּרוּךְ אַתָּה ה׳, מְקַדֵּשׁ הַשַּׁבָּת.

On שַׁבָּת we remember God's goodness in creating the world and caring for all who live in it. On שַׁבָּת we also remember God's greatness in taking our forefathers out of Egypt. That is why, in the קִדּוּשׁ we recite on שַׁבָּת, we find two phrases:

זִכָּרוֹן לְמַעֲשֵׂה בְרֵאשִׁית

זֵכֶר לִיצִיאַת מִצְרָיִם

Write the number of the line that includes זִכָּרוֹן לְמַעֲשֵׂה בְרֵאשִׁית. ——

Write the number of the line that includes זֵכֶר לִיצִיאַת מִצְרָיִם. ——

Different kinds of קִדּוּשׁ

When we recite קִדּוּשׁ on a יוֹם טוֹב, we include the name of the יוֹם טוֹב.
We also add a special phrase to the קִדּוּשׁ.

holidays and times for gladness   חַגִּים וּזְמַנִּים לְשָׂשׂוֹן

Here is a קִדּוּשׁ we recite on a specific יוֹם טוֹב.

1 בָּרוּךְ אַתָּה ה׳ אֱלֹהֵינוּ מֶלֶךְ הָעוֹלָם,

2 אֲשֶׁר בָּחַר בָּנוּ מִכָּל עָם וְרוֹמְמָנוּ מִכָּל לָשׁוֹן,

3 וְקִדְּשָׁנוּ בְּמִצְוֹתָיו.

4 וַתִּתֶּן לָנוּ, ה׳ אֱלֹהֵינוּ, בְּאַהֲבָה,

5 מוֹעֲדִים לְשִׂמְחָה, חַגִּים וּזְמַנִּים לְשָׂשׂוֹן,

6 אֶת יוֹם חַג הַמַּצּוֹת הַזֶּה, זְמַן חֵרוּתֵנוּ

7 מִקְרָא קֹדֶשׁ, זֵכֶר לִיצִיאַת מִצְרָיִם.

8 כִּי בָנוּ בָחַרְתָּ וְאוֹתָנוּ קִדַּשְׁתָּ מִכָּל הָעַמִּים

9 וּמוֹעֲדֵי קָדְשֶׁךָ בְּשִׂמְחָה וּבְשָׂשׂוֹן הִנְחַלְתָּנוּ.

10 בָּרוּךְ אַתָּה ה׳, מְקַדֵּשׁ יִשְׂרָאֵל וְהַזְּמַנִּים.

1 Which line includes the name of the holiday? ________________

2 What holiday is named? ________________

3 Why is Passover ''the time of our freedom''? ________________

____

4 Why is a holiday called a יוֹם טוֹב? ________________

____

5 שָׂשׂוֹן means *gladness, joy*. Write another Hebrew word you have learned that means *happiness, joy*. ________________

הַשְׁכִּיבֵנוּ

God protects us in many, many ways. The הַשְׁכִּיבֵנוּ prayer asks God to continue to protect us every day. Practice reading this תְּפִלָה.

1 הַשְׁכִּיבֵנוּ יְיָ אֱלֹהֵינוּ לְשָׁלוֹם. וְהַעֲמִידֵנוּ מַלְכֵּנוּ לְחַיִּים.

2 וּפְרוֹשׂ עָלֵינוּ סֻכַּת שְׁלוֹמֶךָ. וְתַקְּנֵנוּ בְּעֵצָה טוֹבָה מִלְפָנֶיךָ:

3 וְהוֹשִׁיעֵנוּ לְמַעַן שְׁמֶךָ.

4 וְהָגֵן בַּעֲדֵנוּ וְהָסֵר מֵעָלֵינוּ אוֹיֵב דֶּבֶר וְחֶרֶב וְרָעָב וְיָגוֹן.

5 וְהָסֵר שָׂטָן מִלְפָנֵינוּ וּמֵאַחֲרֵינוּ.

6 וּבְצֵל כְּנָפֶיךָ תַּסְתִּירֵנוּ כִּי אֵל שׁוֹמְרֵנוּ וּמַצִּילֵנוּ אָתָּה.

7 כִּי אֵל מֶלֶךְ חַנּוּן וְרַחוּם אָתָּה.

8 וּשְׁמוֹר צֵאתֵנוּ וּבוֹאֵנוּ לְחַיִּים וּלְשָׁלוֹם מֵעַתָּה וְעַד עוֹלָם.

9 וּפְרוֹשׂ עָלֵינוּ סֻכַּת שְׁלוֹמֶךָ.

10 בָּרוּךְ אַתָּה יְיָ הַפּוֹרֵשׂ סֻכַּת שָׁלוֹם עָלֵינוּ. וְעַל כָּל עַמּוֹ יִשְׂרָאֵל וְעַל יְרוּשָׁלָיִם:

1 Cause us, O Lord our God, to lie down for the night in peace, and
   in the morning awaken us, our King, to life again.
2 Enfold us with the shelter of Your peace, and improve us
   with Your good counsel.
3 Help us, for You are a merciful God.

4 Shield us against foe, and plague, and sword, and famine, and grief.

5 Liberate us from evil powers that assail us on every side.

6 Shelter us by Your Presence, for You, O God, are our
   Guardian and Deliverer.
7 You, O God, are a gracious and merciful King.

8 Guard our going out and our coming in for life and peace,
   now and forever.
9 May You enfold us with the shelter of Your peace.

10 Praised are You, Lord, who spreads peace over us, over all Your
   people Israel, and over Jerusalem.

1 Copy the Hebrew line that asks God to guard our going out and
   our coming in and to give us life and peace.

____

____

2 Write the Hebrew clue words that helped you find this line.

guard ___________________   peace ___________________

life ___________________   forever ___________________

83

HERE ARE SOME WORDS IN
Lesson Twelve

בָּנוּ	בָּחַר	זֵכֶר	בֶּאֱמֶת	צוֹדֶק
	בּ-ח-ר	ז-כ-ר		צ-ד-ק

In each סִדּוּר phrase on this page you will find at least one of these familiar words, or one that is related to it (has the same root). Practice reading these phrases. Then complete the exercises on the next page.

1 זֵכֶר רַב טוּבְךָ יַבִּיעוּ, וְצִדְקָתְךָ יְרַנֵּנוּ

2 צַדִּיק ה׳ בְּכָל דְּרָכָיו, וְחָסִיד בְּכָל מַעֲשָׂיו

3 קָרוֹב ה׳ לְכָל קֹרְאָיו, לְכֹל אֲשֶׁר יִקְרָאֻהוּ בֶּאֱמֶת

4 כִּי בָנוּ בָחַרְתָּ וְאוֹתָנוּ קִדַּשְׁתָּ מִכָּל הָעַמִּים

5 תּוֹרַת אֱמֶת נָתַן לְעַמּוֹ אֵל

6 אֲשֶׁר בָּחַר בָּנוּ מִכָּל הָעַמִּים וְנָתַן לָנוּ אֶת תּוֹרָתוֹ

7 וּזְכַרְתֶּם אֶת כָּל מִצְוֹת ה׳ וַעֲשִׂיתֶם אֹתָם

8 לְמַעַן תִּזְכְּרוּ וַעֲשִׂיתֶם אֶת כָּל מִצְוֹתָי, וִהְיִיתֶם קְדֹשִׁים לֵאלֹהֵיכֶם

9 בָּרוּךְ אַתָּה ה׳ אֱלֹהֵינוּ מֶלֶךְ הָעוֹלָם, אֲשֶׁר בָּחַר בִּנְבִיאִים טוֹבִים

וְרָצָה בְדִבְרֵיהֶם הַנֶּאֱמָרִים בֶּאֱמֶת.

10 בָּרוּךְ אַתָּה ה׳, הַבּוֹחֵר בַּתּוֹרָה וּבְמֹשֶׁה עַבְדּוֹ...

וּבִנְבִיאֵי הָאֱמֶת וָצֶדֶק.

1 Find and circle three words on the opposite page that belong to the ז־כ־ר word-family.
On which lines did you find them? #— #— #—

What meaning do these words share? _________________

2 Circle three words that belong to the צ־ד־ק word-family.

On which lines did you find them? #— #— #—

What meaning do these words share? _________________

3 Phrases #7 and #8 include the words מִצְוֹת and מִצְוֹתַי.

What is a מִצְוָה? _________________

Prayers that tell us about God

Read each תְּפִלָה and then write the subject of the תְּפִלָה in English. (Even if you don't know every word, you know enough *important* words to understand the basic meaning of the תְּפִלָה.)

1 עֹשֶׂה שָׁלוֹם בִּמְרוֹמָיו, הוּא יַעֲשֶׂה

שָׁלוֹם עָלֵינוּ וְעַל כָּל יִשְׂרָאֵל

____

2 אַהֲבָה רַבָּה אוֹתָנוּ אֲהַבְתָּנוּ

____

3 גָּדוֹל ה׳ וּמְהֻלָּל מְאֹד וְלִגְדֻלָּתוֹ אֵין חֵקֶר

____

4 בָּרוּךְ שֶׁנָּתַן תּוֹרָה לְעַמּוֹ יִשְׂרָאֵל בִּקְדֻשָׁתוֹ

____

5 שׁוֹמֵר ה׳ אֶת כָּל אֹהֲבָיו

____

6 כִּי שֵׁשֶׁת יָמִים עָשָׂה ה׳ אֶת הַשָּׁמַיִם

וְאֶת הָאָרֶץ

____

These תְּפִלוֹת tell us one of the following:

_____ God is great

_____ God brings peace to the world

_____ God loves us

_____ God is the Creator

_____ God protects us

Write the number of the תְּפִלָה next to each English statement.

What do these תְּפִלוֹת say?

You know all, or almost all, the words in these תְּפִלוֹת. Read each one and write its meaning in your own words. If there is one word that you don't know, try to guess its meaning in the whole phrase.

1   הָאֵל הַמֶּלֶךְ הַגָּדוֹל וְהַקָּדוֹשׁ בַּשָּׁמַיִם וּבָאָרֶץ

____

____

2   כִּי מִצִיוֹן תֵּצֵא (will come out) תוֹרָה וּדְבַר ה׳ מִירוּשָׁלַיִם

____

____

3   אַהֲבַת עוֹלָם בֵּית יִשְׂרָאֵל עַמְּךָ אָהַבְתָּ

____

____

4   כִּי ה׳ הוּא הָאֱלֹהִים בַּשָּׁמַיִם מִמַּעַל (above) וְעַל הָאָרֶץ מִתַּחַת

____

____

5   עֶרֶב וָבֹקֶר בְּכָל יוֹם תָּמִיד (always), פַּעֲמַיִם (twice) בְּאַהֲבָה "שְׁמַע" אוֹמְרִים

____

____

6   וּבְטוּבוֹ מְחַדֵשׁ בְּכָל יוֹם תָּמִיד מַעֲשֵׂה בְרֵאשִׁית

____

____

A daily — An occasional בְּרָכָה

Some בְּרָכוֹת can be said very frequently — sometimes every day. Others can be recited from time to time. Still others are said only once or twice a year on a special occasion.

Here are the endings of 8 בְּרָכוֹת. Next to each one write F for *frequently*, O for *once in a while*, S for a *special occasion*.

1 הַמּוֹצִיא לֶחֶם מִן הָאָרֶץ ———

2 בּוֹרֵא פְּרִי הַגָּפֶן ———

3 בּוֹרֵא מִינֵי מְזוֹנוֹת ———

4 בּוֹרֵא פְּרִי הָעֵץ ———

5 בּוֹרֵא פְּרִי הָאֲדָמָה ———

6 לִשְׁמֹעַ קוֹל שׁוֹפָר ———

7 לְהַדְלִיק נֵר שֶׁל חֲנֻכָּה ———

8 לְהַדְלִיק נֵר שֶׁל שַׁבָּת ———

9 עַל אֲכִילַת מַצָּה ———

10 עַל נְטִילַת יָדַיִם ———

CHALLENGE QUESTIONS

1 Without seeing the beginnings of these בְּרָכוֹת (which would give you the answer), can you explain the difference between the first 5 and the last 5?

———

2 Some of these בְּרָכוֹת are said only at home. Others may be said at home or in בֵּית הַכְּנֶסֶת. One בְּרָכָה is said *only* in בֵּית הַכְּנֶסֶת. Write the last three words of that בְּרָכָה.

———

When is it said? ———

The priestly blessing

Over 2,000 years ago, when there was a Temple in יְרוּשָׁלַיִם, the priests, כֹּהֲנִים, used to bless the people. The בְּרָכָה they pronounced is still recited in בֵּית הַכְּנֶסֶת.

This is the blessing said by the priests. It is called בִּרְכַּת כֹּהֲנִים.

May the Lord bless you and protect you

יְבָרֶכְךָ ה׳ וְיִשְׁמְרֶךָ

May the Lord shine His face upon you
and be gracious to you
May the Lord lift His face to you

יָאֵר ה׳ פָּנָיו אֵלֶיךָ וִיחֻנֶּךָּ

יִשָּׂא ה׳ פָּנָיו אֵלֶיךָ

And give you peace.

וְיָשֵׂם לְךָ שָׁלוֹם.

Did the priests in the Temple in Jerusalem compose this בְּרָכָה? No — it is even older than the Temple! It is found in the תּוֹרָה which tells us that this was the בְּרָכָה recited by Aaron, the brother of Moses, when he blessed בְּנֵי יִשְׂרָאֵל during their travels in the desert.

1 Write the Hebrew words that ask God

a) to protect you _______________________

b) to be good to you _______________________

c) to respond to your prayers _______________________

d) to bring peace to your life _______________________

2 Think of someone whom you love, and write a blessing for him or her, using your own words. You might wish to ask other things of God.

אֵין כֵּאלֹהֵינוּ

אֵין כֵּאלֹהֵינוּ אֵין כַּאדוֹנֵינוּ
אֵין כְּמַלְכֵּנוּ אֵין כְּמוֹשִׁיעֵנוּ.
מִי כֵאלֹהֵינוּ מִי כַאדוֹנֵינוּ
מִי כְמַלְכֵּנוּ מִי כְמוֹשִׁיעֵנוּ.
נוֹדֶה לֵאלֹהֵינוּ נוֹדֶה לַאדוֹנֵינוּ
נוֹדֶה לְמַלְכֵּנוּ נוֹדֶה לְמוֹשִׁיעֵנוּ.
בָּרוּךְ אֱלֹהֵינוּ בָּרוּךְ אֲדוֹנֵינוּ
בָּרוּךְ מַלְכֵּנוּ בָּרוּךְ מוֹשִׁיעֵנוּ.
אַתָּה הוּא אֱלֹהֵינוּ אַתָּה הוּא אֲדוֹנֵינוּ
אַתָּה הוּא מַלְכֵּנוּ אַתָּה הוּא מוֹשִׁיעֵנוּ.

יִגְדַּל

יִגְדַּל אֱלֹהִים חַי וְיִשְׁתַּבַּח נִמְצָא וְאֵין עֵת אֶל מְצִיאוּתוֹ.

אֶחָד וְאֵין יָחִיד כְּיִחוּדוֹ נֶעְלָם וְגַם אֵין סוֹף לְאַחְדוּתוֹ.

אֵין לוֹ דְמוּת הַגּוּף וְאֵינוֹ גוּף לֹא נַעֲרוֹךְ אֵלָיו קְדֻשָּׁתוֹ.

קַדְמוֹן לְכָל דָּבָר אֲשֶׁר נִבְרָא רִאשׁוֹן וְאֵין רֵאשִׁית לְרֵאשִׁיתוֹ.

הִנּוֹ אֲדוֹן עוֹלָם וְכָל נוֹצָר יוֹרֶה גְדֻלָּתוֹ וּמַלְכוּתוֹ.

שֶׁפַע נְבוּאָתוֹ נְתָנוֹ אֶל אַנְשֵׁי סְגֻלָּתוֹ וְתִפְאַרְתּוֹ.

לֹא קָם בְּיִשְׂרָאֵל כְּמֹשֶׁה עוֹד נָבִיא וּמַבִּיט אֶת תְּמוּנָתוֹ.

תּוֹרַת אֱמֶת נָתַן לְעַמּוֹ אֵל עַל יַד נְבִיאוֹ נֶאֱמַן בֵּיתוֹ.

לֹא יַחֲלִיף הָאֵל וְלֹא יָמִיר דָּתוֹ לְעוֹלָמִים לְזוּלָתוֹ.

צוֹפֶה וְיוֹדֵעַ סְתָרֵינוּ מַבִּיט לְסוֹף דָּבָר בְּקַדְמָתוֹ.

גּוֹמֵל לְאִישׁ חֶסֶד כְּמִפְעָלוֹ נוֹתֵן לְרָשָׁע רָע כְּרִשְׁעָתוֹ.

יִשְׁלַח לְקֵץ יָמִין מְשִׁיחֵנוּ לִפְדּוֹת מְחַכֵּי קֵץ יְשׁוּעָתוֹ.

מֵתִים יְחַיֶּה אֵל בְּרֹב חַסְדּוֹ בָּרוּךְ עֲדֵי עַד שֵׁם תְּהִלָּתוֹ.

מַה טֹבוּ

מַה טֹבוּ אֹהָלֶיךָ, יַעֲקֹב, מִשְׁכְּנֹתֶיךָ יִשְׂרָאֵל.

וַאֲנִי, בְּרֹב חַסְדְּךָ, אָבֹא בֵיתֶךָ,

אֶשְׁתַּחֲוֶה אֶל הֵיכַל קָדְשְׁךָ בְּיִרְאָתֶךָ.

יְיָ, אָהַבְתִּי מְעוֹן בֵּיתֶךָ, וּמְקוֹם מִשְׁכַּן כְּבוֹדֶךָ.

וַאֲנִי אֶשְׁתַּחֲוֶה וְאֶכְרָעָה, אֶבְרְכָה לִפְנֵי יְיָ עֹשִׂי.

וַאֲנִי תְפִלָּתִי לְךָ יְיָ, עֵת רָצוֹן,

אֱלֹהִים, בְּרָב חַסְדֶּךָ, עֲנֵנִי בֶּאֱמֶת יִשְׁעֶךָ.

קְדוּשָׁה

נְקַדֵּשׁ אֶת שִׁמְךָ בָּעוֹלָם כְּשֵׁם שֶׁמַּקְדִּישִׁים אוֹתוֹ
בִּשְׁמֵי מָרוֹם כַּכָּתוּב עַל יַד נְבִיאֶךָ. וְקָרָא זֶה
אֶל זֶה וְאָמַר:
קָדוֹשׁ קָדוֹשׁ קָדוֹשׁ יְיָ צְבָאוֹת
מְלֹא כָל הָאָרֶץ כְּבוֹדוֹ.
אָז בְּקוֹל רַעַשׁ גָּדוֹל אַדִּיר וְחָזָק מַשְׁמִיעִים קוֹל.
מִתְנַשְּׂאִים לְעֻמַּת שְׂרָפִים לְעֻמָּתָם בָּרוּךְ יֹאמֵרוּ:
בָּרוּךְ כְּבוֹד יְיָ מִמְּקוֹמוֹ.
מִמְּקוֹמְךָ מַלְכֵּנוּ תוֹפִיעַ וְתִמְלֹךְ עָלֵינוּ כִּי מְחַכִּים
אֲנַחְנוּ לָךְ. מָתַי תִּמְלֹךְ בְּצִיּוֹן בְּקָרוֹב בְּיָמֵינוּ
לְעוֹלָם וָעֶד תִּשְׁכֹּן. תִּתְגַּדַּל וְתִתְקַדַּשׁ בְּתוֹךְ
יְרוּשָׁלַיִם עִירְךָ לְדוֹר וָדוֹר וּלְנֵצַח נְצָחִים. וְעֵינֵינוּ
תִרְאֶינָה מַלְכוּתֶךָ כַּדָּבָר הָאָמוּר בְּשִׁירֵי עֻזֶּךָ
עַל יְדֵי דָוִד מְשִׁיחַ צִדְקֶךָ:
יִמְלֹךְ יְיָ לְעוֹלָם אֱלֹהַיִךְ צִיּוֹן לְדוֹר וָדוֹר. הַלְלוּיָהּ:

שִׂים שָׁלוֹם

שִׂים שָׁלוֹם טוֹבָה וּבְרָכָה חֵן וָחֶסֶד וְרַחֲמִים עָלֵינוּ וְעַל כָּל יִשְׂרָאֵל עַמֶּךָ. בָּרְכֵנוּ אָבִינוּ כֻּלָּנוּ כְּאֶחָד בְּאוֹר פָּנֶיךָ. כִּי בְאוֹר פָּנֶיךָ נָתַתָּ לָנוּ יְיָ אֱלֹהֵינוּ תּוֹרַת חַיִּים וְאַהֲבַת חֶסֶד וּצְדָקָה וּבְרָכָה וְרַחֲמִים וְחַיִּים וְשָׁלוֹם. וְטוֹב בְּעֵינֶיךָ לְבָרֵךְ אֶת עַמְּךָ יִשְׂרָאֵל בְּכָל עֵת וּבְכָל שָׁעָה בִּשְׁלוֹמֶךָ. בָּרוּךְ אַתָּה יְיָ הַמְבָרֵךְ אֶת עַמּוֹ יִשְׂרָאֵל בַּשָּׁלוֹם.

שָׁלוֹם עֲלֵיכֶם

שָׁלוֹם עֲלֵיכֶם מַלְאֲכֵי הַשָּׁרֵת מַלְאֲכֵי עֶלְיוֹן.
מִמֶּלֶךְ מַלְכֵי הַמְּלָכִים הַקָּדוֹשׁ בָּרוּךְ הוּא.
בּוֹאֲכֶם לְשָׁלוֹם מַלְאֲכֵי הַשָּׁלוֹם מַלְאֲכֵי עֶלְיוֹן.
מִמֶּלֶךְ מַלְכֵי הַמְּלָכִים הַקָּדוֹשׁ בָּרוּךְ הוּא.
בָּרְכוּנִי לְשָׁלוֹם מַלְאֲכֵי הַשָּׁלוֹם מַלְאֲכֵי עֶלְיוֹן.
מִמֶּלֶךְ מַלְכֵי הַמְּלָכִים הַקָּדוֹשׁ בָּרוּךְ הוּא.
צֵאתְכֶם לְשָׁלוֹם מַלְאֲכֵי הַשָּׁלוֹם מַלְאֲכֵי עֶלְיוֹן.
מִמֶּלֶךְ מַלְכֵי הַמְּלָכִים הַקָּדוֹשׁ בָּרוּךְ הוּא.

אַשְׁרֵי

אַשְׁרֵי יוֹשְׁבֵי בֵיתֶךָ עוֹד יְהַלְלוּךָ סֶּלָה.

אַשְׁרֵי הָעָם שֶׁכָּכָה לּוֹ אַשְׁרֵי הָעָם שֶׁיְיָ אֱלֹהָיו.

תְּהִלָּה לְדָוִד

אֲרוֹמִמְךָ אֱלוֹהַי הַמֶּלֶךְ וַאֲבָרְכָה שִׁמְךָ לְעוֹלָם וָעֶד.

בְּכָל יוֹם אֲבָרְכֶךָּ וַאֲהַלְלָה שִׁמְךָ לְעוֹלָם וָעֶד:

גָּדוֹל יְיָ וּמְהֻלָּל מְאֹד וְלִגְדֻלָּתוֹ אֵין חֵקֶר.

דּוֹר לְדוֹר יְשַׁבַּח מַעֲשֶׂיךָ וּגְבוּרֹתֶיךָ יַגִּידוּ.

הֲדַר כְּבוֹד הוֹדֶךָ וְדִבְרֵי נִפְלְאֹתֶיךָ אָשִׂיחָה.

וֶעֱזוּז נוֹרְאֹתֶיךָ יֹאמֵרוּ וּגְדֻלָּתְךָ אֲסַפְּרֶנָּה.

זֵכֶר רַב טוּבְךָ יַבִּיעוּ וְצִדְקָתְךָ יְרַנֵּנוּ.

חַנּוּן וְרַחוּם יְיָ אֶרֶךְ אַפַּיִם וּגְדָל חָסֶד.

טוֹב יְיָ לַכֹּל וְרַחֲמָיו עַל כָּל מַעֲשָׂיו.

יוֹדוּךָ יְיָ כָּל מַעֲשֶׂיךָ וַחֲסִידֶיךָ יְבָרְכוּכָה.

כְּבוֹד מַלְכוּתְךָ יֹאמֵרוּ וּגְבוּרָתְךָ יְדַבֵּרוּ.

לְהוֹדִיעַ לִבְנֵי הָאָדָם גְּבוּרֹתָיו וּכְבוֹד הֲדַר מַלְכוּתוֹ.

מַלְכוּתְךָ מַלְכוּת כָּל עֹלָמִים וּמֶמְשַׁלְתְּךָ בְּכָל דֹר וָדֹר.

סוֹמֵךְ יְיָ לְכָל הַנֹּפְלִים וְזוֹקֵף לְכָל הַכְּפוּפִים.

עֵינֵי כֹל אֵלֶיךָ יְשַׂבֵּרוּ וְאַתָּה נוֹתֵן לָהֶם אֶת אָכְלָם בְּעִתּוֹ.

פּוֹתֵחַ אֶת יָדֶךָ וּמַשְׂבִּיעַ לְכָל חַי רָצוֹן.

צַדִּיק יְיָ בְּכָל דְּרָכָיו וְחָסִיד בְּכָל מַעֲשָׂיו.

קָרוֹב יְיָ לְכָל קֹרְאָיו לְכֹל אֲשֶׁר יִקְרָאֻהוּ בֶאֱמֶת.

רְצוֹן יְרֵאָיו יַעֲשֶׂה וְאֶת שַׁוְעָתָם יִשְׁמַע וְיוֹשִׁיעֵם.

שׁוֹמֵר יְיָ אֶת כָּל אֹהֲבָיו וְאֵת כָּל הָרְשָׁעִים יַשְׁמִיד.

תְּהִלַּת יְיָ יְדַבֶּר פִּי וִיבָרֵךְ כָּל בָּשָׂר שֵׁם קָדְשׁוֹ לְעוֹלָם וָעֶד.

וַאֲנַחְנוּ נְבָרֵךְ יָהּ מֵעַתָּה וְעַד עוֹלָם. הַלְלוּיָהּ.

When you began your textbook and this workbook, you recited this בְּרָכָה:

בָּרוּךְ אַתָּה ה׳, אֱלֹהֵינוּ מֶלֶךְ הָעוֹלָם,
שֶׁהֶחֱיָנוּ וְקִיְּמָנוּ וְהִגִּיעָנוּ לַזְּמַן הַזֶּה.

Now you have finished your textbook and this workbook.
And now you can recite what all Jews say when they finish a Book
of the תּוֹרָה:

חֲזַק חֲזַק וְנִתְחַזֵּק!